One Man's War

Robert Allison

DEDICATION

In Loving Memory

Robert H. Allison

December 19, 1921 – March 18, 2010

CONTENTS

FORWARD

This book is a chronicle of my father's experiences as a navy fighter pilot during WWII. He began writing a personal history for his family in the mid 1990's. I can't say what inspired him. I just noticed one day he was writing, initially in long hand. We got him onto a computer and he was off and running. I don't believe my father was bored or looking for something to occupy his time. He had already been retired for ten years and had settled into a life of golf and volunteer work with the local police department. Not being a writer he was a bit self-conscious initially, using a disparaging working title of "The Boring Saga of One Man's War". He was not a pretentious person and I believe he was concerned that we, his family, would think he was making too much of long ago memories. To us, it's a treasure.

I'm struck by the amazing detail my father was able to pull from memory. There are names, places, and dates from over 50 years ago. He is recalling all of this when he was in his mid seventies.

I remember hearing most of the incidences described in this book many times as I was growing up. They read as I remember hearing them, with my dad's eye for the ironic, something I have learned from him. I remember them being told with a smile, usually because they involved some funny misadventure. But, I can't help wondering now if in some part, it was just the relief that it was over and in the past. Not all of his squadron mates returned from the war.

I am amused at his casual outlook looking back to those days. It's not exactly how I remember him as a father. I don't know that his attitude actually changed over the years. I suspect he felt the freedom to be himself in these writings, not having to present a parental image to a young boy. I think he was conscious when I was young of how his attitude might shape mine and was more guarded about things like portraying authority in a bad light. Similarly, some stories of blatantly irresponsible horseplay on the part of himself and his buddies are new to me. Reading these stories takes me back. I can hear his voice in these pages. It's probably the closest connection to him that I have now that he is gone.

Hearing these stories as a kid, I never had a time scale or sense of order of events. It seemed that he had a million stories about flying all over the US as if he was part of a huge boondoggle. I realize now that the Navy spent two years training my father before sending him overseas. Between November of 1942 and December of 1944 he was training and logged over 600 hours as a pilot. I find this incredible considering that Army Air Corps pilots were flying bombers over Europe with just a handful of hours as pilots. Why the huge training disparity? At the end of 1942, the US only had two aircraft carriers. I believe the navy needed this time to build up a fleet of ships that could carry the war to the pacific. During that time, many navy pilots trained in the US. By contrast, there were bases in England that the army could use to fly over Europe immediately upon our entering the war. The consequences were horrible for those early army pilots and aircrews. By the time my father got to the fighting we had superior weapons in vastly superior numbers. By the end of the war, the US had built over 150 aircraft carriers. Because he always made it sound like fun to a young kid, I never saw the serious side nor did I realize that he participated in over fifty combat missions.

I'm still fascinated reading about his two failed carrier takeoffs. He was the photo reconnaissance pilot in his squadron and had access to the ship's photo lab. He lifted five of the ship's official photographs, complete with "Confidential" stamps on the back, showing his progress down the flight deck and over the side into the ocean. I have included these pictures in this book. Destroyers picked him from the ocean and traded him back to his squadron in exchange for a bucket of ice cream on both occasions. He used to joke about this, complaining that his "hide" was worth more than a bucket of ice cream.

My dad describes meeting my mother for the first time. The initial attraction, as I heard when I was young, was that my mother owned a car, a rare charm indeed during the war. An early draft of this story had them meeting in a bar. This later morphed into "restaurant", I think my mother's doing. My mother jointed the Army Nurse Corps after my father went overseas. She is always happy to point out that she eventually out ranked him before they both left the service.

I was sure my father's account of the war as he saw it would interest others outside our family. I posted the story on the internet and quickly received a number of gratifying responses. Many people wrote to thank him for sharing his experiences. Several people had lost loved ones during the war and had always wondered what they went through. There were those, also, with family members who returned from the war but never talked about it. My father was contacted for an interview for an oral history project and was interviewed by a couple of high school kids for class projects. My father got an enormous kick out of reading his guestbook entries. I wish I could thank everyone who posted messages.

In a completely unexpected turn, we were contacted by the Museum of Flight in Seattle. Through the navy, they had tracked the bureau number of an aircraft they were restoring to my father's squadron and then to my father through his story on the web. They asked if he knew anyone who might have flown their aircraft or had pictures showing squadron markings to aid in the restoration. We checked my dad's flight log which shows he flew their particular aircraft on two occasions in the western Pacific in April, 1945. It's quite a coincidence that sixty plus years ago my father flew into combat one of the handful of FM2 Wildcats still in existence today. We traveled to Seattle for a reunion. My father had a great time telling the restoration crew all about the war and seeing his plane once again. It was a wonderful experience, my special thanks to the crew at the Museum of Flight.

My father succumbed to cancer on March 18, 2010 at the age of 88. This book says so much about who he was. I can't think of a more fitting tribute or better way to preserve his memory for future generations of his family than to publishing this work. Maybe, future generations will find insight as well, into the lives of the youth of his generation, who found themselves involved in a world war.

My father lived through a momentous period in history. It is hard to imagine a conflict on such a scale occurring now days, thank goodness. The kids of that era had to grow up quickly but being part of something so much bigger than themselves gave them a unique perspective. I believe it's a perspective that subsequent generations can't understand or appreciate.

Was this the greatest generation as Tom Brokaw maintains? I don't know. But one can certainly argue that they witnessed the most sweeping changes in civilization and participated in the most monumental events in the history of mankind.

Robert C. Allison, 2012

Robert H. Allison

1

PRE-WORLD WAR II TO DECEMBER 7, 1941

I would like to make mention of the fact, before I get into this high adventure story and I mean "High" as in altitude not in exploits and deeds, that before the war, the highest perch I was ever on was the eighteenth floor of the Equitable building in Des Moines looking over the parapet at the street below. I was terrified of leaning on the parapet looking down the side of the building. Even today I am very uneasy leaning on a metal rail looking down into the Grand Canyon. I had no idea how I would react to being several thousand feet high in a plane. From the first flight I had, I was completely at ease even when hanging upside down at all altitudes with nothing but a safety belt between me and the ground several thousand feet below. I'm sure it was because of my faith in the belt, but also the fact that I always had a parachute strapped to my butt. The only times I flew without a parachute was when I was riding in a passenger plane. Passenger planes never bothered me.

This is no attempt at being the author of a best selling novel nor a high adventure fiction tale of a brave and courageous hero but an actual and truthful accounting of an average nineteen year old high school graduate caught up between a rock and a hard place of a raging world war, who, if he didn't choose into which service he was going to serve his country, he would most likely be drafted in the Naval service as a seaman second class or in the Army as a buck-ass private.

You may think as you read through this autobiography that this guy lived a life of faux pas and was a disaster waiting to happen. But if you take into consideration the total amount of faux pas time as compared to the total amount of flying time, the bad times and the hair raising times, whether due to pilot error or not, probably did not account for more than about one percent of my time in the air over this three year period. What you will not read in this story is an accounting of my daily, routine flights where nothing worthy of note happened even though to me they were exciting experiences.

I don't believe at that time I even considered being a marine. The thought never crossed my mind. Nor, for sure, did I consider joining the Hooligan Navy (Coast Guard). It was my opinion at that time anyone joining the Coast Guard was looking for a soft spot in some comfortable seaport in the United States where he was not likely to get his ass shot off. That might have been true in some cases. But, in fact, they were very likely to wind up piloting a landing craft onto some unknown beach in the pacific in the face of withering gunfire.

The reasoning that was to be instrumental in influencing my selection of the Navy as a branch of the service in which I was most interested began several years before the United States intervened in the World War II.

Sometime during my early teens my two brothers, Melvin and Carl, and I were greatly interested in aeroplanes and the exploits of World War I aviators and the adventures of radio heroes such as "Jimmy Allen", "Jack Armstrong", and "Curly, Slim, and Tubby" and "Captain Midnight" and other radio programs and movie serials. We spent many hours at the Des Moines airport watching the small planes take off and land, dreaming that we were one of those adventuresome souls at the controls of those planes. Every summer we would go to the Iowa State fair to watch the barnstorming pilots do acrobatics and take up passengers. It was never our good fortune to be one of those passengers. It was, at that time, a dream that we would very likely not ever experience.

In my early years I made a vow that if the United States ever got into another conflict and I were called upon to serve my country that the army would teach me to fly. I could well imagine myself doing rolls, loops and being another Eddy Rickenbacker. But time passed and I grew away from these boyhood dreams and began thinking about what I would be doing the rest of my boring life.

I was graduated from Abraham Lincoln High School in January 1940. After a couple of uninteresting, temporary jobs I went to work for Central National Bank in Des Moines in June 1940. It was a job, which at that time, was not easy to come by and was very low pay. I did not believe that this would be my life's career. The only reason for mentioning this job is that it was the connection between my civilian life and the military.

2

DECEMBER 7, 1941-- JULY 8, 1942
ATTACK ON PEARL HARBOR

It was during this time that Pearl Harbor was attacked on December 7, 1941. At the time of the attack on Pearl Harbor, which was about two o'clock p.m. Iowa time, my brother, Carl, and I and two of our friends, were about ten miles out in the country doing a little target practice with our 22 caliber rifles. It was on our way home that we heard over the car radio of the attack on Pearl Harbor. We were highly incensed that anyone would have the guts to pick a fight with our Navy especially a scrawny little nation like Japan.

We had no doubts that our Army and Navy would mop up the floor with Japan and in no time. We were especially irritated because our brother, Melvin, was in the Navy and was stationed in Pearl Harbor aboard the cruiser, USS Raleigh, at that time. For the next two weeks we did not hear from Melvin, but then learned that he had not been injured even though the Raleigh, which was tied up at Ford Island at the time, took a 500 pound bomb on the stern that passed through the ship, through his golf clubs and exploded in mud.

That Sunday we had no idea of the devastation to the US fleet caused by the attack; nor that a major part of the Pacific fleet lay on the bottom of Pearl Harbor. Nor were we aware that about 3000 service men had been killed and many more had been wounded.

In the next few days after the declaration of war with Japan, Germany and Italy on December 8th there was a mobbing of the local recruiting stations with patriotic young men trying to volunteer. This was in addition to those who were being drafted by the selective service agency. I was not one of them. Not because I was not patriotic but because I had a recurring vision of fulfilling my teenage dream of having the Army teaching me to fly an airplane.

Working with me at the bank were two young guys about my age who had signed up to take a refresher course in some of the subjects that would help them pass the Army Air Corps entrance exam. For me it sounded like a good idea. The course was offered by the local Elks Lodge who had hired two Drake University students to teach these courses in math, history, english grammar and a few other subjects they thought were necessary for passing the test.

Here was an opportunity to improve my chances of becoming a pilot and doing it the way I said I would years earlier, that is: at the army's expense. I hadn't forgotten the desire. So I took advantage of the BPOE and, indeed, I owe them a debt of gratitude. For three months I attended these classes three nights a week.

In March, the Army Air Corps was to give a test for aviation cadets. I was prepared to take it when my brother, Carl, decided to come home from Washington, D.C., where he had been working for the FBI in the finger print department. He wanted to take the test too. When he found out the Elks were starting another class, he decided he would attend the refresher course. So we both waited while he took the course.

3

JULY 8, 1942 -- NOVEMBER 15, 1942
ENLISTING IN THE V-5 PROGRAM

Near the end of his course the Navy was giving a preliminary test for a

Naval Aviation Cadet program (V-5 NavCad Program) at the Des Moines

recruiting station. We decided to take a stab at this test before the Army

gave theirs, which was scheduled a couple of weeks later. We did and we

both passed the written, oral and physical exams. A few days later we

received train tickets and orders to report to the Naval Aviation Cadet

Selection Board in Kansas City, Missouri on July 8, 1942. We reported on

the date given for the written, oral and physical exams that literally

dwarfed the tests given in Des Moines. Again we both passed and were sworn in to the United States Navy as cadets in the V-5 NavCad program. We were told to return home and wait for orders to report for duty.

For the next four months we waited and I continued to work at the bank. About the first of November, both Carl and I received orders to report for duty on the 15th of November. Carl was ordered to Morningside College in Sioux City, IA, about two hundred miles northwest of Des Moines. I was ordered to Northwest Missouri State Teachers College in Marysville, MO. This town is about 80 miles southwest of Des Moines. So right off the get away we are going different directions together.

The bank I was leaving had adopted a policy of making a bonus donation of $300.00 to all of their employees entering the service. The big catch was that each individual must have put in eight hours a day, forty hours a week for as long as he had been employed. Unfortunately, I, as well as many others, was very short on time, maybe as much as a hundred hours, due to the nature of the work and the fact no one ever said anything when you finished your work and left early. For the last few weeks before leaving I would stay until nine or ten o'clock at night playing cribbage or gin rummy with the other short timers. I made up the time, collected the three hundred dollars and was off to Marysville, MO.

4

NOVEMBER 15, 1942--MARCH 15, 1843
MARYSVILLE, MO
NORFOLK, NE – CPT/WTS

There were twenty Navy cadets in the V-5 program that arrived with me.

The program at that time was known as CPT, or Civilian Pilots Training. A

month later the name was changed to WTS (War Training Service). We

were quartered in the college dormitories. At the school at the time was a

group of Army men who were training to be pilots in the Army Signal

Corps. They would be flying Piper Cub L-5 airplanes for the signal corps.

Their future was flying low and slow spotting for the artillery.

The CPT program consisted of two months of a half-day ground school

and a half-day flight instruction. It was here, a couple of days after I

arrived, that I had the first ride of my life in an airplane. I don't remember my reaction to that ride, whether I was scared or not, but I survived. After eight hours of instruction the instructor crawled out of the front seat and said, "You're on your own". He took his parachute and walked back to the flight line.

Fat, dumb and, I'm sure, not so happy I headed the plane across the field, advanced the throttle, rolled down the field and lifted into the air, a nice smooth takeoff. At about 500 feet I made a left-hand circle of the field, looked down and realized that I was at the point where I was going to have to land. I was up and had to get down. I couldn't change my mind. I made a left hand turn into the final approach, eased the throttle back and gently settled to the ground. I'm not so sure that plane didn't land itself. I took off again and when I was on the down wind leg I looked down and could see the tracks my plane had made on it's first landing in a carpet of snow about six inches thick that had accumulated the night before. The plane left a curving trail that made a ninety-degree turn to the right. I did not realize this was happening on that first landing. At least the snow taught me a lesson about concentration while being at the controls and was probably responsible for the nice soft landing.

Marysville was a fun place, but we had a lot of snow while we were there.

My roommate, whose name was Bill Woods from Saint Jo, MO, was about six foot two and a fresh air fiend. Every night he would open the window as wide as he could. After arguing with him and not winning I gave up and piled on all the blankets I could get a hold of and then slept in my clothes. Several times the floor was covered with snow the next morning.

Another one of that crew was a guy named Pardee, who in the middle of the night, while sound asleep, would sit up in his top bunk, flying his plane just as if it were real. He would wake everybody in the dorm. He was scared to death. He had twelve hours instruction and never soloed. He was washed out of the program.

One of the other guys was from Des Moines. On about the second weekend he and I caught a ride about nine p.m. on Saturday night to a small town about 40 miles north of Marysville, MO and still about 46 miles from Des Moines. From that town we caught another ride to Oseola, IA, about 30 miles from Des Moines and from there another ride to Indianola, IA, sixteen miles south of Des Moines. It was two o'clock Sunday morning and cold as hell. We walked all the way to Des Moines and got home about six o'clock that morning only to have to go back that evening. Only good thing was he drove his car, an old 1925 Star, back to Marysville. From then on we had transportation.

On one cold and snowy Saturday morning this friend from Des Moines, and I took off in his Star heading for Des Moines. To keep the engine from freezing we partially covered the radiator. Somewhere about half way home the radiator boiled over and we had to walk about a mile to a farmhouse to get water for the thing. Needless to say there was no antifreeze in the radiator.

We were once again on this sixteen-mile stretch from Indianola to D.M. when we crossed the crest of a hill and half way down the hill was a semi truck jackknifed on the icy road, stopping traffic in both directions. There was a long line of cars on both sides of the road and nothing was moving. We were sitting, pondering our situation when all of a sudden my friend, the driver, cramped the front wheels to the right and took off through the ditch, out over the frozen snow covered fields, through the creek, past the semi and up the other side of the hill, through the ditch and back on the highway. After getting on the highway I looked back and here was a long parade of cars following the same tracks that we had left behind. That old Star was a pretty good car!

At the end of the two months I had thirty-five hours flying time in the Piper Cub airplane. Of the twenty men who started the V-5 program at Marysville MO, nineteen of them completed it with 35 hours of flying time. The one guy who didn't finish was the guy who would not fly the plane solo. Of the twenty men who were in my brother's class at Sioux City, nineteen completed the course with their 35 hours. The one guy who didn't make the grade was a wise guy who was demonstrating his talents as an aviator to a farmer's daughter he had met in town by hedgehopping in a field behind her house. The wing of the plane struck a haystack and the plane struck the ground ending in a pile of scrap. He walked away from the wreckage and kept right on walking out of the V-5 program.

One hotshot pilot

There were other accidents or injuries in these classes. About the most trouble we could get into other than crashing was to get lost while flying solo. It was an uncomfortable situation to get lost and run out of fuel then landing in some farmer's alfalfa or cornfield. To mow down a long strip of alfalfa or several rows of corn then looking out the side of the plane and see the farmer running toward your plane with a pitchfork can be very disconcerting. Never heard of anyone being tickled with a pitchfork but the part about getting lost and making an emergency landing was certainly not unheard of.

At the end of the two months I had thirty-five hours flying time in the Piper Cub airplane. The program was completed and I received orders to go home and wait.

Carl arrived home from Sioux City at the same time I did with the same orders. Within two weeks we both received orders. They were not for preflight school as we had hoped. In his case the orders were for pre-preflight. Mine were for another WTS program that would last one month and gain me another twenty hours flying time. This time I made a train trip from Des Moines to Omaha, Nebraska, changed to an antique train that had a potbellied stove for heating the passenger car, and because the weather was subfreezing the stove was burning coal and the car was filled

with smoke and soot, for the trip to Norfolk, Nebraska and Norfolk Junior

College.

The accommodations for me and nineteen other guys were in the local

YMCA. Arriving late in the evening and being the first one there, the

manager asked me if I would mind sharing a room with one of the guys in

the preceding class, who would be leaving in a couple days. Assuming that

I would then have a room by myself and that I didn't know any of the new

guys who would be in my class, I agreed. My new roommate was, at the

time, in the big town of Norfolk. I didn't meet him until about midnight

when this loud noise came in with three or four of his buddies and turned

on the lights. They were a drunk, loud and obnoxious bunch of hoods, at

least this guy was. I immediately knew why he didn't have a roommate

before. I had been suckered! He only lasted two days and I did have the

room to myself. Strange thing is that I never saw him again until about

fifteen years after the war had ended, when I was driving home from

work in Wilmington, CA. I saw him standing on the corner of Figueroa and

Pacific Coast Highway. He was still in the service and wouldn't you know, a

Marine! We both recognized each other, or at least we appeared familiar to each other. I gave him a ride to his temporary home in Harbor City and had a nice conversation with he and his wife.

5

MARCH 1, 1943 -- MAY 31, 1943
IOWA PRE-FLIGHT SCHOOL

Bus transportation took us to the University of Iowa campus where we were assigned rooms in the Hillcrest dormitory. Once again being alphabetically number one on the list I was assigned to a four man room in which there was already a cadet from a previous battalion, this was John Horn. John had been in the 16th battalion when he came down with spinal meningitis. He very nearly died but bore it out and was now reassigned to the 20th battalion, company C, 1st platoon. Also in the room the first night was one of my Norfolk classmates, Clyde Clifford Cavitt. The fourth bunk would not be occupied for a couple of days when we were to receive the late arrival of Benjamin J. Moise.

Room mates at Iowa Preflight
Allison, John Horn, Clyde (Cactus) Cavitt

A word or two about my roommates, John Horn was from St. Cloud, Minnesota, a fun loving guy who was as weak as a cat from his sickness. He was so weak that when we had to take a five minute step test he was on the verge of passing out and falling. I was along side of him and was able to support him without being caught by the instructor. Only had one complaint about him; he kept washing his balls in the sink in our room. We kept jawing the hell out of him until he quit. Upon leaving preflight he went to NAS Minneapolis for primary, never heard of him again. Cavitt was from Colfax, Iowa, about sixteen miles from Des Moines. His nickname was Cactus because of his hair. It was thick, coal black and stood straight up on his head like a porcupine. Never saw or heard of him again after preflight. B.J. Moise was from New Orleans, Louisiana. He was the only one of the whole platoon who had not gone to CPT/WTS, which was too bad because if there was anyone who ever wanted to fly it was B.J. B.J. had not been in the V5 program as long as the rest of us because of an accident in which he was involved. While waiting to be called for CPT/WTS, B.J. and a friend of his were out on the beach of the Gulf of Mexico taking target practice on sea gulls with their 22 caliber rifles. B.J. was lying in the sand sighting on a gull and pulled the trigger just as his friend raised up in front of him. The bullet struck his friend in the back of the head. He was killed instantly. B.J. was in such deep depression that his father, an influential man in New Orleans, was able to get the Navy to take him early to help get his mind off the accident. B.J. had been to Tulane University, had taken mathematics through calculus. He, through carelessness, failed a simple math test so badly that they wouldn't even let him take a make up. He was gone. One thing B.J. was good at was aircraft recognition. We were required to be able to identify all military combat aircraft, both the allies planes and those of the enemy from all angles: front, astern, from the sides, top and bottom. Not only identify them but do it in one seventy-fifth of a second. This is about as fast as you can blink. B.J. knew them all. On one test twenty photographs of various planes were flashed on the screen at this speed. Only one cadet of the whole class got twenty right answers- that was B.J. The hooker was that a photo of a cat had been inserted. He was the only one who identified it as an old tomcat. Everyone else had been looking for an airplane.

Preflight school was scheduled for a three-month period of a half-day of ground school and a half-day of physical education, supposedly to sharpen your reflexes, both mentally and physically. Maybe so! Physically maybe it did, but mentally I was still left with a lot to be desired.

The first thing we received was another physical followed by being issued naval cadet uniforms. These were genuine real to goodness officer's uniforms minus the rank stripes. They not only made you look good but gave you an air of confidence and maybe a little or a lot of ego. This was especially true after the uniforms we had been issued in WTS which were the forest greens that were used by the CCC (Civilian Conservation Corps) in the mid thirties. The daily work uniforms (fatigues) the 20th and 21st battalions received were the Army winter olive fatigues with Army boots. All other battalions received marine greens and marine brogans which probably didn't look any better but they didn't make you stand out like a diamond in a goat's butt as the Army uniforms did for us for about a month. New comers were known as "Boots" - we were pegged!

This was basically three months of just plain fun, nothing but every sport in the books, inter-platoon, inter-company, inter-battalion and inter-regimental competitions. Was great! Ground school was not much of a challenge for me. But there were several cadets who fell by the wayside because of it. The only thing that caused me a problem was that I was not able to take Morse code as fast as required, flunked the test first time. So as not to flunk it the second time I conned Cactus Cavitt to taking it for me. We passed with flying colors. If we had been caught we would have still been flying-off the end of a boot. The only time I ever remember taking advantage of a test was in the first physical I took in Des Moines. This was the depth perception test. This was the ability to line up a stationary wooden peg with one that was controlled forward and backward by the use of two strings at a distance of 20 feet. I happened to notice that as the moveable peg passed the stationary one that had a light behind it cast a faint shadow. I used the shadow but it wasn't necessary to do this, I would have passed anyway.

One of the more pleasant things about preflight was the study hour from nine o'clock until "lights out" at ten. Just before nine we would dash down to the ship's service, load up on apples, oranges, crackers and anything else that looked good. Get back to the room and pretend to be studying when the inspecting officer came by. After he had made his check, it was "party time". Well, maybe not party time but it was sure a relaxed, peaceful time of day. Study? Didn't know what the word meant.

Another source of pride and pleasure was each Sunday morning when the entire regiment marched in a parade to the athletic field next to the athletic field house for inspection. There were 2000 cadets in dress blues or in dress whites, in rank and file formation. It was impressive to me and even more so to my mother, father and two sisters, Marilyn, 16 and Helen, 11. They had driven from Des Moines just to witness this parade and attend Navy chapel in the field house following the parade. And I like to believe that maybe, they glowed a little bit with pride for their son and brother. I think I had an ego problem. Besides, one of my mother's friends whose husband happened to be my father's boss and a twin brother to my uncle the husband of my mother's sister, had said to her that neither my brother nor I would make it because it was too tough a grind and we weren't up to it. Because of that "snob" there was no way I was going to

fail.

Allison family minus two brothers

6

JUNE 1, 1943 -- AUGUST 1, 1943
NAS OTTUMWA, IA
PRIMARY FLIGHT TRAINING

Upon the completion of this segment of training we each received orders

to proceed to our next station which was primary flight school. There

were several flight schools in the midwest: NAS Minneapolis, NAS St.

Louis, NAS Olathe, Kansas and NAS Ottumwa, Iowa. We could choose so I

chose NAS Ottumwa. It was only ninety miles from Des Moines and I could

and did take off for home at every opportunity. Des Moines was a great

liberty town for the personnel at Ottumwa in that NAS Ottumwa was the

only military station within several hundred miles with the exception of

Fort Des Moines. Fort Des Moines was the Women's Army Corps

induction center. The town was crawling with unattached young women.

Unfortunately, it was my hometown and I was there to visit my family. It might have been unfortunate, but it was a kick for my sisters as we walked down the street and I would receive an endless supply of salutes from these women soldiers. They were not required to salute since I and the uniform were only a cadets and not entitled to a salute. A cadet wore an officer's uniform but lacked the stripes of rank and a commission. I wasn't going to tell them.

Up until now our training was just a time filler as far as the Navy was concerned. We were considered absolute neophytes as far as flying was concerned. We were starting out from scratch. The program was the same half-day ground school and a half-day flying as we had in WTS. We were quartered in a barracks, 120 cadets on the first floor and 120 on the second. My group was assigned the first floor. Again being alphabetically number one, I caught the top bunk above a guy in the previous class, I think his name was White, which made him last in his class. The only reason for mentioning this is that one night just before "lights out" I was standing up- right on the top bunk and must have bounced because the wires supporting the mattress gave way and I plunged through. There I was standing up to my waist in my mattress with my feet on his mattress. At that moment the lights went out and I spent the remainder of the night sleeping in a hole with my fanny about six inches from this guy's face. The next morning I repaired the springs.

NAS Ottumwa was a new base that had only been open for about a month when we arrived. The field was a large macadam square that served as a runway for a wind that could come from any direction. This was convenient for us fledgling flyers since we would have no cross winds to contend with. The operations buildings and the ready room were small square temporary wooden shacks. In that it was still spring and rains were plentiful, the area around the macadam was a quagmire of mud.

I would guess that there were about 100 N2S's for about three or four hundred students which served pretty good in that four students were assigned to one instructor and he could take up only one at a time. We were limited to one-hour flights so that the four students would each get in one hour of flying in the half of a day on the flying schedule. The N2S was known by other names, such as the "PT-17" for the Army Air Corps, also the "Yellow Peril" because of the bright yellow color for both the Army and Navy. The plane was a biplane and had two, in tandem, open cockpits. It had a 225 HP engine and was very maneuverable. Truly great for acrobatics and as about as safe an airplane as anyone would want.

The training program consisted of five stages. The first stage, as I recall, was familiarization and soloing. The last was formation flying. The "in between" stages were for gaining confidence in the flying and receiving instructions in every thing you could do with the plane, such as slow rolls, snap rolls, loops, split Ss, spins, slips, stalls and a variety of other things including night flying. Also included in these stages were rides with "check" pilots who would either approve your techniques or give you a "down". A "down" was a fail to pass the check and required a second check ride. Another "down" meant that you would have to take extra instruction in that stage. A third "down" and you were on your way home with a future of a new career in the Army or Navy. Although I never considered my self a "Hot Pilot" I never received a "down" in primary flight school. One of the instructors, whose name was Rubishotus, was famous for his "downs". Wouldn't you know he was from Des Moines and graduated from North High School. Luckily, I never got him for a check ride.

My flight in primary consisted of three other cadets, Don Bopp, Charles Coleman, and William Clark. Our instructor's name was Ensign Robert Liggett. He was two or three years older than the four of us and had been in the Navy maybe a year longer than we. He had gone through the flight program, graduated from NAS Pensacola. He was assigned to three months of instructor's school and sent to NAS Ottumwa as an instructor. We were his first students. We all got along fine with Liggett and the flying. Even though I didn't have a "down" as I said before, I came close on "slips to circles". In the process of teaching me to slip a plane to a 100-foot circle Liggett demonstrated a very nice slip and hit the circle square in the center. The he told me to do the same. I made a slip identical to his and hit the circle, not as neat as his but in the circle. He said "great! Now just do the same thing every time." In my practice sessions I wasn't so lucky. When it came to a check for this stage of the program, my "check" pilot jerked off the throttle as we passed along side the circle at an altitude of about 500 feet and said "hit the circle. With an idling engine and losing altitude rapidly I banked into the field lined up on the circle, place the plane in a slip and just short of the circle and about 15 feet in the air I kicked the plane out of the slip expecting to hit the circle in the center. Not to be, the plane ballooned and we sailed right across the circle and touched down well beyond the circle. The "check pilot" yelled out "Good God!" who taught you to slip like that". He said, "Now I'm going to show you how to slip a plane after which you get to try to slip to six circles. If you hit three of the six I'll give you an "up", if you don't, you get a "down!" In his demonstration, he made his approach to the field and as he lined up on the circle he pulled the nose above the horizon, pushed hard on the right rudder and held the control stick hard left to keep the left wing down giving the plane a descending approach at an angle to the field. The plane was just above stalling speed and shaking like a dog excreting razor blades. At the last moment he kicked the plane square with the line of flight. The plane hit the circle like a ton of bricks. I had just learned how to slip to a circle. He landed the plane, got out, said: "try your luck! Pick me up when you're through". I did, hit three, got my "up" and again never had any trouble with slips to circles, small field procedures, nor "check" pilots in primary after that. All that was required to do the slips right was to make a "rock" out of the plane and let it drop- a controlled drop, that is!

Another stage of our training was night flying. It's really no different than day flying except that on a really black, overcast night you can't see anything. If you are lucky enough to have stars or the lights from a town or a farmhouse you can survive. If you don't have any lights or a horizon then you are on instruments-needle, ball, air speed, a compass and an altimeter. With these you can survive, but it takes training. We didn't have nor would we get instrument training until we reached Pensacola.

Therefore, it was spooky as hell when we had our training in the dark of the moon.

For night flying, a runway was laid out on the macadam square with two rows of flare pots running parallel to each other and about fifty feet apart and always into the wind. On my first experience at night flying, after I had taxied to the end of the so-called "runway", I received the green light to go, advanced the throttle and immediately the plane veered to the left. By the time I got the plane straightened out, the plane was running straddle of the left line with the flares squarely between the wheels of the plane. Rather than taking a chance on hitting a flare pot while trying to get back between the two rows, I just held the plane straight until it had enough speed to lift off the ground. If I had damaged the plane, that would have been the end of my flying days.

One of the dangers of night flying was vertigo. That is a dizziness that is experienced by staring at a single point of light on a dark night. To avoid vertigo you have to keep shifting your eyes constantly. I don't know what would have happened those days of primary training without instrument training. A pilot subject to vertigo would lose control of the plane and spin in. Night flying wasn't especially fun as far as I was concerned.

Running between Des Moines and Ottumwa was the Des Moines River on its way to the Mississippi River. This was a stretch of 90 miles as the crow flies or about 200 miles of "S" turns as a snake crawls. There was one guy in our platoon who had been a roommate of Don Bopp in pre-flight and was of the same conceited nature as Bopp, a "Hot Pilot". One day, on one of his solo flights, he was getting his "Jollies" by skimming just above the water making "S" turns between the trees. What he didn't see was this electric cable stretched between two poles on either side of the river. The cable caught the wheels of his training plane and flipped it on its back in the river. The guy got out of the plane and swam to shore with his parachute on his back. Was picked up, returned to the field, reported to the flight office, was discharged and was on his way home that afternoon. The administration was somewhat considerate of errors but was completely intolerant of horseplay and foolishness.

In the service you meet very few people you knew in civilian life. This happened to me on only three occasions during my time in the service. The first time was here at Ottumwa. One day a whole bunch of us cadets were getting on one of the cattle cars (buses that ferried people around the station) when I suddenly recognized the sailor who was driving the bus. It was a guy by the name of Clifford Anderson. He and I entered kindergarten at Park Avenue elementary school and were in the same homerooms and classes in every grade and graduated together. I was surprised to find him driving a bus because he was not only a fairly bright guy but was a first string halfback on our high school football team. He was also a good-looking guy and quite the ladies man. Needless to say, I was quite envious of him in high school. On several occasions when I had the time I would jump in the cab with him and ride around the station discussing good old times.

The only time I was ever in the hospital was here at Ottumwa. In pre-flight I had gotten blisters on the back of both my legs where the tops of my boots constantly were rubbing. The blisters turned into nasty sores and after a couple of months I went to sick bay to have them treated. They not only treated the sores but also kept me in bed for three days.

Every time a person arrives at a station or leaves a station he is given a physical and a dental check. When I was checking out of Ottumwa I was told that I had about five minor cavities which the dentist filled. Upon arriving at Pensacola I was checked and told I had several minor cavities and these were also filled. I didn't have guts enough or brains enough to ask what the hell was coming off. My guess is that these dentists were getting in a lot of practice at the expense of a bunch of defenseless cadets. We suspected that our squadron doctor operated at the drop of a complaint just to keep his hand in. There were very few calls for surgery with a bunch of healthy young men.

7

AUGUST 1, 1943 -- JANUARY 25, 1944
NAS PENSACOLA, FL -- BASIC, INSTRUMENT,
ADVANCED FLIGHT TRAINING
AND GRADUATION

And so, after successfully completing both the ground school and the five

stages of flying, we boarded a train for an over night ride from Ottumwa,

Iowa to Pensacola, Florida. The pullman we were assigned to had one less

bunk than the number of cadets assigned to it. The odd guy without a

bunk turned out to be John August Munson, a CPT/WTS student who had

been at Morningside College in Sioux City with my brother, Carl. He and

his buddy, Gene Rife, another guy from Sioux City, had managed to get to

the train last and Munson didn't get a bunk. So wouldn't you know since I

had the lower bunk and Rife an upper, Munson piled in with me. In those days homosexuality wasn't on everybody's mind and no one thought anything of two men sleeping in the same bunk. Not so today!

Our destination in Pensacola was the Pensacola Naval Air Station, the "Annapolis of the Air". This is one of the two final squadrons, the other being Corpus Christi Naval Air Station, where half the Navy cadets who have completed primary schools around the United States, and even some cadets from foreign countries, come for the final stages of their training before becoming full fledged Naval Aviators, presented their "Wings of Gold" and are commissioned as Ensigns in the United States Navy by proclamation of the Congress of the United States of America. To me and to everyone else it was no small honor. This I assure you!

Once we were checked into NAS Pensacola we were assigned to one of two out lying stations for basic training. These stations were Sauffley field and Ellison field, both named after early naval aviation heroes. I drew Ellison. It was the usual half-day ground school and half-day flying.

The planes we would be flying were the PT- 19, Vultee Valiant or the Vultee Vibrator as the cadets called it. In the Navy it was known as the SNV. It was an all-metal, low-winged monoplane, considerably heavier than the Stearman with a little more horsepower. It, too, was a two seat, in tandem plane with a radio in place of the "gosport" arrangement in the Stearman. One stipulation on the plane was that, as far as the Navy was concerned, it was not constructed for acrobatics and as far as stunts were concerned, -no dice. The Army Air Corps had no such restrictions.

GREETINGS FROM
PENSACOLA, FLORIDA
HOME OF
U. S. NAVAL AIR STATION

The required postcard for the folks back home

Basic training was a short course designed to make a transition from the Stearman to a more combat like plane, the SNV. Here again the SNV was not a hard plane to fly but that didn't stop me from getting into trouble. My first "faux pas" occurred when I was taxing out to the end of the runway with my instructor and another cadet for a three-plane formation takeoff. During the taxi out the pilot has to lower the flaps. This requires twenty-eight turns of the flap crank. I was in the process of cranking when I had to throttle back to keep from over running the plane ahead. Beings you use the same hand for cranking and jockeying the throttle, I paused in the cranking after 14 turns of the 28 necessary. When I continued cranking I cranked 14 turns in the opposite direction, hence, no flaps, a situation I was unaware of. On the run down the runway the wingmen are suppose to lift off before the flight leader, in this case the instructor. We were rolling along at what seemed to a very low speed. I couldn't lift the plane off the runway. All of a sudden the instructor poured to juice to his plane and I did the same. We left the other plane dragging way behind. Once we were in the air the instructor gave a hand signal that my flaps were up. I instantly knew that was the reason my plane was heavy. It doesn't require nearly as much air speed to raise a plane with flaps as it does without. The instructor was rather understanding about my explanation of counting. I didn't find that my error was necessarily a dangerous one in that the takeoff was accomplished without any difficulty even though we had used up a good portion of the runway before the instructor looked back and saw my predicament. I was rather amused when a few days later I was reading the Pensacola paper and saw a picture of Ted William's, the Boston Red Sox baseball player, and read how he narrowly missed death when he took off in his SNV with the flaps up. A newspaper will print anything for news. Not only was the story "bullshit", but in the picture "ole" Ted had the epaulets on his dress white uniform snapped on upside-down. Not only did I read it, but someone else pinned the picture to the bulletin board in the barracks.

I'm not saying that is the only error I made. On one of my check rides I was to make practice landings. The instructor, whose name I believe was Lt. (j.g.) Weiss, told me to make the approach at 90 knots. My air speed ran between 85 and 95 knots. I couldn't control the speed because of the rough air. Maybe it was because of the rough air and maybe not. Anyway, the "ass" flew into a rage because of my lack of "ability". Berated me up one side and down the other side, told me I was too dumb to be a Navy flier and gave me a "down". I would gladly have killed the "Son of a Bitch" on the spot.

Once we were back on the field I met with my instructor and was so depressed that I made the mistake of saying that I might as well quit! Something that influenced a rash statement like this was the fact that an order came out stating that any cadet who remained in the program after the 3rd of September would no longer be able to resign from the Navy but would go directly Great Lakes Training Station as a seaman second class. Those who desired not to accept this would be released from the program and returned to civilian life as of this date. The third of September just happened to be the next day. The instructor said "I wish you hadn't said that, I would have given you extra time, but now I would hold myself responsible if anything happened to you. But, if you wish, I will try to get you board time". Now I was in a predicament, do I go or do I stay. At any other time there would be no question, I could take the board time and if I failed I could get out. But not now, that evening I had a pocket full of quarters, puzzling over whether I should make the call home telling them I was a quitter. Well, I never made the call, the instructor got me the board time and I never looked back. What piss-poor timing! I have never forgiven that horse's ass Weiss.

From basic all cadets went to Whiting field, another out-lying field, for instrument training. It was a relatively short course for learning to fly on instruments and to study navigation including celestial navigation. Flying a plane under a hood makes you blind to the outside world and you are forced to control the plane on instruments. Don't know how well I did with the blind flying but I didn't crash and I did pass the check. I must have learned something for I was called upon to use these techniques many times later on.

One of the two other things I remember about NAS Whiting was sitting in a classroom with the only other fellow American cadet by the name of Allen. He was the other cadet in the three-plane takeoff at NAS Ellison who was left on the runway. Also in the class were 18 Sub-Lieutenants of the British Royal Navy who were here for the same reason as the USA cadets-to learn to fly. Sitting in the classroom with my mind somewhere on "cloud nine" the instructor suddenly asked me "What is the most dangerous situation you can get into in an airplane?" Not having really heard the question, I was stumbling over the question and the answer when I heard one of the Sub-lieutenants whisper "a flat spin." I repeated the whispered answer to the instructor and again escaped by the skin of my teeth. Since that time I have a warm place in my heart for the Royal Navy. A few years later as I was reminiscing about the past, I began to wonder why I didn't know and why I should have had any reason to be embarrassed because I was not familiar with the term "flat spin". To the best of my knowledge I had never heard of the term and it had not been a term used in courses of flying or ground school, either in lectures or in textbooks. As for textbooks, I think I'm safe in saying that I was never issued a textbook all the time I was in the Navy. One would think that a flying instructor would have mentioned it with the idea of promoting safety or that it would have been a part of the "Theory of Flight" or in the lectures on aircraft construction and maintenance. Don't remember hearing the words until I was asked that question. So would I have been reprimanded for not knowing the answer? Maybe not. For anyone who doesn't know the meaning of the term and might be interested, it is this: An airplane is designed and constructed with a center of gravity point along the longitudinal axis of the fuselage of the airplane. This means that the weight forward of this point is exactly equal to the weight aft. It would balance perfectly on a fulcrum. The plane is constructed with the weight a little heavier on the forward half. The reason for this is so that in case of engine failure the nose will fall first there by gaining speed and increasing the wind over the control surfaces. If the after-section of the plane were heavier the tail would fall quickest and the pilot would not be able to gain control of the aircraft there by spinning to earth.

To compensate for the uneven weight distribution the elevators on the horizontal stabilizer are fitted with small trim tabs. These are small elevators that can be adjusted by the pilot to maintain level flight without maintaining pressure on the stick at all speeds.

The other thing about our stay at Whiting all cadets were required to purchase a full set of officers uniforms or have their cadet uniforms altered and fitted with stripes. The only guy I knew that had his uniforms altered was Jim Wells (I'll get to him later). By the time we had been sold our dress blues, dress whites, khakis, greens, hats and shirts, we were in debt some two or three hundred dollars, for which the clothing companies in Pensacola were willing to trust you - the Navy would see that they got their money. Three hundred dollars sounds like a real bargain price today but at that time it was a fortune.

Before ordering uniforms all cadets were given the opportunity to go into Marine aviation or stay with the Navy so that the ones desiring the Marine Air Corps could order Marine uniforms. A small percentage did choose and became Marines. These guys like to spread the word that the Marine Corps took only the top ten percent of the cadets for the Marines. That's "BULL SHIT". It would be correct to say that the Marines took only the top ten percent of those who applied. They could have been in the top ten but that 10 percent of those who applied could have been the bottom 10 percent of the whole class. Most likely they were spread through out the whole regiment.

At this time we were also given the opportunity for choosing the type of flying we would like to do after graduation: fighters, bombers, torpedo planes, observation planes, flying boats, multi-engine or lighter-than-air. I chose fighters and got my choice, maybe because my name began with "A". Those choosing to be Navy fighter or bomber pilots were sent to NAS Baron Field. The P-boat pilots and the Marines went to NAS Bronson Field and all others went to the main station, NAS Pensacola.

Baron Field had the nick name "Bloody Baron" because of the number of casualties it had accumulated due to the red dust that penetrated everything including the engines. There were many crashes because of engine failures. There was a story going around that at one time there were twelve bodies stretched out on the hanger floor, awaiting boxes for shipment. I'm sure it was "bull" because the Navy wouldn't permit anything as crude and demoralizing as that. I think it is fair to say that the field didn't get its name from the "Red Baron" Von Ricktoffen either.

This was our final squadron. The planes we were to fly would be the North American SNJ, or as the Army called it, the AT-6, or as the English called it, the "Harvard". It was a great training plane and there are many flying yet today, 50 years later. It was the first plane I flew that had retractable landing gear and mounted a .30 caliber machine gun in the cowling that fired through the propeller arc. Firing the machine gun at a towed target was probably the only new type flying we would do; everything else was just rehash, practice and polish.

I don't remember my roommates at Ellison field but I do at Baron. I again wound up on the top bunk. Underneath me was John Burns, a red headed Scotsman from Pennsylvania. Nice guy, a couple of years older than the rest of us in the room. He was completely fascinated with the poem "High Flight" composed by an RAF fighter pilot who was killed in the battle for Britain. John could recite the poem from end to end and often did. On the other side of the room in the lower bunk was Don Bopp, whom as I have already mentioned as one of my three flight mates at NAS Ottumwa. He was a guy with an over abundance of self-confidence. The kind of a guy we liked to refer to as a "Hot Pilot". They may or may not be, but he, in my opinion, was just an average guy, neither great nor bad.

On the top bunk over Bopp was Tom Bloski. It turned out that Tom and I would be roommates at our next station. Writing home was a worth while past time and Tom was good at it. He had written to his mother that he had good roommates that he liked. One was a Catholic like himself, one was a Lutheran, which isn't much different than a Catholic and the third one was a Protestant who didn't go to church. His mother wrote back to say that it was nice he had good roommates even if one was a Heathen. We didn't have any doubts as to whom she meant. However bad I am, my father wasn't a "Bootlegger" from East Chicago, Indiana!

One thing the Navy had was lots of inspections and parades. Every Saturday we would muster on the street in front of the barracks then march to the parade ground in our dress blues or dress whites, which ever the weather dictated, there the base commander would hold inspection. I never received any demerits even though I only shaved every three or four weeks whether I needed it or not. One Saturday Bloski and I decided that we wouldn't stand inspection. We got Burns and Bopp to answer the roll call when the platoon mustered in front of the barracks. We went into a janitorial closet under the stairwell to avoid the officer who checked the rooms for guys like us. Fortunately, the checker didn't check the broom closet and after he left we went back to room and waited for the others to return. The commanding officer was pretty liberal with the demerits and wouldn't you know both Burns and Bopp each got a demerit. We thought that was pretty funny -- might have been but if we had been caught we would have spent a year in flight training for nothing. Looking back, it was pretty dumb.

Flying the SNJ was a great deal of fun. As each stage of our training came up the size of the plane would get bigger. By the time we had reached the SNJ we felt pretty "hot" and were ready to take on the world.

We completed our final squadron course at Baron Field on January 24, 1944 and returned to the main station. On January 25, 1944 in full dress uniform with about 200 other cadets on parade, we were commissioned as Ensigns in the United States Navy or 2nd Lieutenants in the United States Marines by an act of the Congress of the United States. At the same time we were presented with "Wings of Gold" and issued certificates that designated us as "Naval Aviators". We had arrived. Nothing could take that away from us but a general court marshal or death.

8

JANUARY 25, 1944 -- MAY 1, 1944
NAS GREEN COVE SPRINGS, FL
OPERATIONAL FLIGHT TRAINING

Bloski and I received orders to report to Green Cove Springs Naval Air Station near Saint Augustine, Florida. We received 6 days travel time to go about two hundred miles. What to do with 6 days? We decided to go to New Orleans. Even though it was in the wrong direction it wasn't far and we had neither been there before. Good idea! Besides, it would give me a chance to find out what had happened to B.J. Moise.

We bought bus tickets, boarded the bus, walked to the seat that crossed the back of the bus and flopped. There was lots of room and besides there were only about five people on the whole bus. The bus didn't move. The driver just sat there in his seat and kept looking in the rear view mirror at us. Finally he got up came back and said: "You boys will have to move forward. This section is reserved for the "Colored". OK! We moved forward. This was my first, last and only experience with "Jim Crow". We arrived safely in New Orleans with no further incidents.

I knew that B.J.'s parents lived in the Roosevelt Hotel and that his father was president and general manager of Maison-Blanche Department Store in New Orleans. So this was the place to start. We entered the store and asked a clerk where we might find Mr. Moise. She directed us to the offices on the second floor. At the end of the hall was an office door that bore the name: Benjamin J. Moise, President/General Manager. We entered to find in the first office, Mr. Moise's secretary. We introduced our selves. She picked up the phone and in an instant we were sitting in this gigantic office talking to B.J.'s father. After a few minutes he called his secretary and asked her to find his wife - she was in the store. In a couple of minutes she was in the office treating us like long lost kin. I would have to say they couldn't have been more accommodating. Mrs. Moise invited us and insisted upon showing us the town. She called for her car and upon leaving the store we were to enter a big long black limousine which she drove. After picking up B.J.'s sister we were treated to lunch at Antoine's then shown every point of interest in New Orleans from the "French

Quarter, Bourbon Street, the cemeteries where everyone is buried in vaults above ground because it is not possible to keep the bodies under ground because of the water level, and also a trip to Lake Pontchartrain. The answer to my quest of B.J.'s fate was that he had left the Navy and had been drafted as a buck private in the Army. We were invited to dinner but had begged off because of another commitment. Wasn't true but they didn't know. We were more interested in Bourbon Street. After two days in New Orleans we were off to Green Cove Springs.

Walt Glista, Mike Michaelich, Robert Allison,
William Touhimaa, Harry Bates, Sy Gonzalez, Tom Bolski

As student officers, Bloski and I, being numbers one and three on the alphabetical list, were assigned as roommates again. Don't know why I didn't draw Bates. There were seven students in our flight, five of whom I hadn't met before. They were Harry Bates, Walt Glista, Sy Gonzalez, Mike Michelich and Bill Tuohimaa. Bloski was also in the Flight. The instructor we were assigned to was Lieutenant Quentin Crommelin. . He was a full Lieutenant, a graduate of the Naval Academy and had been on sea duty as a gunnery officer prior to entering flight school. No experience in combat as a pilot and he was teaching us how to kill and not be killed.

There is an interesting story about Lt. Crommelin. Not only was he a graduate of the Naval Academy but he was the youngest of five brothers who were all graduates of the Naval Academy. The eldest, Captain John Crommelin was an Aviator and was on the USS Liscome Bay, CVE 56, when it was sunk by a Japanese U-boat in the South Pacific Ocean. He survived. Second was Commander Charles Crommelin, who died in combat as a fighter pilot.

Third, a Lieutenant commander, whose name I don't remember, was the captain of a destroyer. Fourth, Lieutenant Commander Richard Crommelin, also an aviator who flew back to his carrier in a damaged plane with his body racked with shrapnel and one of his eyes hanging on the outside of his cheek. He landed but couldn't control the plane. It crashed into the bridge of the carrier. He survived only to become a fatality in a mid-air collision with another Navy plane during the Okinawa campaign. The fifth and youngest was our instructor.

The Crommelins were true Southerners from Alabama. One day, our instructor arranged for us to go to the skeet range where we were to learn to lead a moving target when shooting at it. Everything was going along fine until a mockingbird made the mistake of landing on a fence on the side of the skeet range. Bates couldn't resist the temptation. He blasted that bird into guts and feathers. The Lieutenant blew his stack and we were off to the B.O.Q. Someone came up with the idea that the mockingbird is the Alabama state bird. Well, maybe so, but I believe his attitude had a little something to do with safety.

Another incident involved with gunnery practice was on the pistol range. There were about 40 or 50 student officers lined up on the pistol range, each with a .45 caliber automatic pistol facing the targets. The instructor in charge gave the command: "ready on the right!, ready on the left!, ready on the firing line!", and before he could get out the word "fire" a shot rang out followed by the words "give that man ZERO FUKO". It was my roommate Bloski. Whenever anyone would pass Bloski after that, in place of saying Hi!, they would say to him: "Give that man ZERO FUKO".

One evening after dinner, Bates and Bloski got to throwing water on each other. It eventually developed into a full-scale war between Bates and Glista's room and ours. Water soon soaked the hallway. After things settled down and Bates and Glista were in bed, Bloski and I took the water filled fire extinguisher off the wall crept down to their door threw it open and emptied the extinguisher on both of them right in the middle of their beds. We dropped the extinguisher and ran for our room locking the door behind us. Our room was on the second floor. In a few minutes we could hear noises in the attic. Bates and Glista had gotten another extinguisher and were crawling through the attic to where they figured they were right over our room. The next thing we knew they had punched a hole in the ceiling and were pumping water down on us. My bed was not hit too badly but Bloski's was soaked. At some time, Sy Gonzales and Bill Tuohimaa had gotten involved but somehow Michelich was left out. He was in his room (a single, no roommate) sound asleep. The six of us filled a condom with a couple of gallons of water. Carefully cradling it in our arms we carried it into his room with the intention of laying it in bed beside him. Unfortunately, as we tried to hold it out over the bed it broke. He was fit to be tied but there wasn't much he could do about it. The four rooms and the hallway were a mess and water was running down the staircase to the lobby.

Even though the "big game" was over the incident was not closed. The next afternoon when we returned from the flight line we found an order for the entire student body, not just the seven of us but all students, were to muster in front of the administration building at 1700 hours. Once there the whole regiment received a tongue lashing by an irate Marine Major, who warned the entire student body that any further acts of vandalism would result in a summary court marshal for the perpetrators for willful destruction of government property. We were not singled out even though we knew that they knew who the guilty parties were.

Another incident involving my friend Bloski concerned a young lady that I had met while with Bates and Glista in a nearby town. This woman was very cute but unfortunately married to a pilot who was at that time flying in the South Pacific. He, also, had been a buddy to another pilot whom had gone to the same high school as I but was in a grade behind me (small world!). My high school friend had been killed in the crash of a B-25 bomber in Texas. This woman and her husband escorted his body back to Des Moines for the funeral. Anyhow, as far as I was concerned, this woman was a very loyal and dedicated wife and she was not for the picking. "Not so!" says Bloski, they can all be made. Give me her name, address and telephone number and on my next liberty I'll show you". A bet was made and he was off. The day he returned from his next liberty he was claiming he had spent the night with her in a hotel. I can't say for positive whether he was telling the truth, but he confessed to me that he was a little worried and whipped out his tool and "lo and behold" the end of it was about three times what it's normal size should have been. The only advice I could give him was "go to sick-bay!". He did and the doctor told him not to worry that the muscle in the foreskin had retracted and cut off circulation to the skin on the wrong side. The doctor pushed the swollen skin back under the retracted muscle and told Bloski to stick around, he was going to be circumcised and was. He spent the next three days in the hospital. The bet was conceded to him.

The assignment to operational training was for the purpose of introducing a student pilot to a genuine, honest to God combat airplane. In this case the Grumman F4F Wildcat. This plane had been the number one carrier based fighter aircraft until the introduction of the Grumman F6F Hellcat and the Vought F4U, Corsair. The F4F remained an operating combat plane until the end of the war but had been relegated to CVEs (Escort

56

Carriers) because of the inability of the F6F and the F4U to operate from the small carriers. At this time we had no idea as to which one of the three planes we would wind up flying in combat.

The first thing I remember about flying the F4F was that it was a single seat plane and that I would have no instructor riding along on my first flight. A couple of things that I learned on the preflight familiarization class was that it took 28 turns of a crank to wind up the wheels after takeoff and that prior to starting your run for takeoff it was necessary to tighten the friction screw on the throttle to prevent the vibration of the plane under full power from causing the throttle to creep back while you cranked up the wheels. It was kind of familiar because the 28 turns of the crank reminded me of the SNV and its flaps. So on my first takeoff I opened the throttle all the way released the brakes and after gaining enough speed I lifted the plane in the air. Having gotten off the ground about 20 feet high I released the throttle, reached down and began cranking and counting. To do this requires that you bend over and you can no longer see where you are going. After about half the turns I raised up to take a peek. To my surprise I saw that the plane was nearly back on the ground and headed for the trees at the end of the runway. By the sound of the engine I knew that I had lost power and immediately realized that I hadn't tightened the friction screw. I gave the engine full power and cleared the trees by not much. If I had cranked those wheels all the way up without looking I would have plowed into the trees.

Another part of the flight training was firing machine guns at a towed target. A fighter plane is basically a flying gun platform, in the case of the F4F, four 50 caliber machine guns. The guns were stationary and arranged two in each wing firing forward and bore sighted so the projectiles from the four guns will converge at a point seven hundred feet a head of the plane. For our practice sessions and to conserve on ammunition the four guns were loaded with 100 rounds each. To aim the guns there is a gun sight mounted behind the wind shield and on top of the instrumental panel directly in front of the pilot making it possible for the pilot to draw a bead on his objective and hit it with machine gun fire. The gun sight is marked off lighted rings that are calibrated in mils from the center to the outside ring. Using these markings makes it possible for the projectiles to hit the target. To hit an enemy plane from a high speed, high angle run it is necessary to get about a 90 mil lead on your prey.

When we had gunnery practice one of the students would be assigned to tow the target and the other six and the instructor would make firing runs until their ammo was exhausted or the target was shot off. At the end of the flight we would gather around the sleeve and count holes. The tip of the round was painted a different color for each of the planes for identification. If we were lucky we would find 1 or 2 or 3 or 4 or maybe 8 or even 10. That is a very few holes for 2800 rounds of ammo. Impressive? Not very! Not to worry! I would learn later. Don't know if the rest of my flight learned to shoot at a later time or not. Don't mistake these gunnery runs with the movies where the "HOT PILOT" sucks in behind the enemy and blows him full of holes. Any "macaroon" can do that. Basically, our lack of knowledge and skill was another case of the instructor not knowing any more than the students.

It was here at Green Cove Springs that we began our training in the technique of carrier landings. There was no carrier near the air station so, as with all other operational schools, an out lying field was marked with the outline of a carrier deck with the location of the arresting wires painted on the deck. The LSO's (Landing signal officer) platform was also outlined in its proper place. We were instructed on making a routine approach by flying upwind at about 500 feet of altitude. About a quarter mile ahead of the painted carrier deck we were to make a 90 degree left turn and let down to 100 feet of altitude, continue cross wind (that is 90 degrees to the course of a carrier sailing into the wind) to about a quarter of a mile to the left and ahead of the "carrier" make a 90 degree left turn and fly down wind. At a point opposite the LSO we were to make a left turn letting down to about fifty feet of altitude. We continue this cross wind approach to a point about 30 degrees off the course of the "carrier". There we begin a turn into the stern of the "carrier".

At this point the LSO picks you up with his paddles and directs your plane into a landing aboard the "carrier" by making motions with the paddles. He will tell you the attitude of your plane and what corrections are required to make to pick up an imaginary wire and make a safe landing. It is absolutely essential that you follow the instructions of the LSO to the letter. It has been proven by experience that he knows your flying speed and attitude in the groove better than you do. Try to out guess him and there's a good chance you will die.

The reason I'm describing this procedure is for relating the only accident experienced by a member of our flight at Green Cove Springs. On one of the several circles for practice landings, Walt Glista, on a left hand turn and let down, stalled his plane and spun in from about 500 feet. He crashed in a field of tree stumps, tore the plane into a mass of twisted wreckage. He walked away unhurt. I don't believe he was even reprimanded-- he finished the program with the rest of us.

As for this stage of the program, flying close to stalling speed and just above the tree tops, was a little spooky at first. After getting use to this way of flying, I really began to enjoy it. The real McCoy was yet to come, that is, landing on a moving, tossing, rolling carrier flight deck.

Night flying wasn't much different except for formation flying. The only thing about formation flying was finding the planes after taking off. On a black night all you could see were the running lights of the planes and you had to find your own division quickly or try to select your flight out of all the other planes in the air. Sometimes it was a crowded sky.

One thing I got a kick out of was making passes at trains that traveled up and down the coast. Not much to it but it was exciting to come down from a couple of thousand feet as hard as the plane would go, level off just above the tracks and head right into the headlight of the train, then pull up at the last second and skin down the length of the train. Doubt very much that engineer even knew we were there. He might have heard the noise, though.

9

MAY 1, 1944 -- MAY 8, 1944 NAS GLENVIEW
CARRIER QUALIFICATION --USS SABLE, (IX81)

Operational training finally came to an end and we considered our selves

ready to meet the enemy. Not to be! Before this could happen the seven

of us received orders to report to NAS Glenview at Glenview, Illinois for

carrier qualification aboard a genuinely real carrier. In our case it would

be the USS Sable, one of two carriers, the other being the USS Wolverine.

Both were land locked in Lake Michigan.

These were two former Great Lakes passenger ships fitted with flight

decks just for the purpose of qualifying neophyte aviators. The Wolverine

had a stern paddle wheel and the Sable had two paddle wheels, one on

either side of the ship.

To qualify as a carrier pilot it was necessary to make eight landings aboard a carrier. Due to the backlog of pilots who were delayed and waiting their turn at qualifying because of bad weather, it took us a week to get our call. On the seventh day we took off from Glenview and flew out over Lake Michigan to the carrier. The first sight of the Sable gave me the feeling that "this can't be for real". That ship looked incredibly small. It might have been a little more comforting if I'd had the opportunity to go aboard the ship first so that I could have gained a feeling for the size of the flight deck.

Well, there was no turning back now —"faint heart never buggered fair lady". So I took my place in the traffic circle and the first thing I knew I was making a turn into the stern of the ship. I picked up the LSO and before I could even think about it I had taken a cut, had hit the deck and was jerked to a stop faster than you can say "Jack Robinson". I didn't even have time to get confused. The confusion was soon enough in coming. I looked out the side, there was a deckhand waving his arms, making motions with his hands and moving his lips in a menacing manner.

After a few seconds I began to interpret all this mumbo-jumbo and began to react. I responded to the signals to release the brakes so the plane would roll backward making it possible for them to release the tail hook, turn up the engine to full power and leave. I did! The roll down the deck wasn't exactly straight and being that the forward end of the flight deck curved a little bit toward the center line of the ship I lifted the plane off the deck just before it ran over a white rope that was about six inches high and running up the side of the flight deck. I actually took off over the side of the ship. I made the seven additional landings without screwing up. Looking back on the first landing, it probably wasn't the best they had ever seen but I'm willing to bet it wasn't the worst. For that matter there were several planes and pilots lost in Lake Michigan over the years that these two carriers were in operation.

From Glenview the seven of us received orders to report to the Naval Air Station at Norfolk Virginia. We were given seven days to get there, so I decided to make a relatively short side trip to Des Moines to "show-off" my "Wings of Gold" to my family and friends. Actually there weren't too many of my friends still at home, only those at the bank where I had been working before going into the Navy. Anyhow, my family was impressed.

10

MAY 1944 -- JULY 1944
NAS NORFOLK, VA -- PHOTO RECONN SCHOOL, HARRISBURG, PA,
NAS NORTH ISLAND, SAN DIEGO, CA

At the naval air station in Norfolk, VA, the seven of us met again. We were

to be at this station for only a week during which time we did no flying.

We were there for reassignment to another station. Upon receiving these

orders we found that the group was being broken up. Bates, Glista and I

received orders to report to Harrisburg, PA, for photo reconnaissance

school. Bloski and the others were to report to the naval air station at

Martha's Vineyards, MA where they would join a squadron. Theirs was a

full fledged squadron, flying F6F's and would be attached to an Essex class

carrier. We did not know at the time that the three of us after photo

school would be flying FM-2's and would be in a composite squadron aboard escort carriers. I later wondered if I would have rather been with the other four guys and the fast fleet and enjoyed their notoriety or if I'm satisfied with the way things turned out. The answer: I think I would have rather have been with the fast fleet. But we did our part and quite effectively and I'm still here and I am rather pleased with our contribution to the war effort.

F6F Hellcat – Photo recon school, Harrisburg, PA

Harrisburg was not a naval air station but just a school established at the Cumberland, PA airport. There was a small detachment of student officers there. Some fighter pilots, some torpedo plane pilots and some dive bomber pilots. The planes we were to fly were F6F's, TBF's and SB2C's. All were equipped with cameras mounted in the fuselage of the planes. We were to learn how to take photographs of the terrain around Harrisburg which would prepare us for serving our future squadrons as the "photo reconnaissance" pilots. It would be our duty to make high and low flying passes over enemy territory taking pictures for use by the Navy intelligence department. This course lasted for only one month which didn't give much time for visiting the local area. Washington, D.C., Philadelphia, and New York were not too far away. I never made any of them. Didn't even make the Hershey candy factory a short way from Harrisburg although I did make it to Harrisburg a few times.

Glista's home was in Massachusetts. On his first day off he took off for his home and returned with his car, a 1936 Ford touring sedan. From then on he and Bates could always be found in Harrisburg when not attending class or flying. One day while the rest of our class were doing our required athletics on an open field, who should go by in the Ford with it's top down but Bates and Glista. The officer in charge saw them, they got their butts reamed out but no further discipline happened. Bates and Glista continued their errant ways.

Flying the F6F in photo school was quite a treat after the F4F. The F6F being the newest Grumman fighter was considerably larger with a 2000 HP engine (800 HP more than the F4F) and faster. Besides it had hydraulically operated retractable landing gear. One photographing trip I engaged in was to the Civil war battleground at Gettysburg, PA. I could see the monuments but not being familiar with the topography I was not able to understand what I was seeing. I regret not keeping the aerial photographs that I took that day.

After a very enjoyable month at Harrisburg, the three of us were ordered to NAS North Island in San Diego. This time instead of a train I was treated to a flight on United Airlines. I booked passage on a DC-3 with a stop over in Des Moines. The flight to Des Moines had two stops, one in Indianapolis, IN and one in Chicago. When the plane was about to leave Indianapolis about ten of us were asked to leave the plane to make room for about ten Army pilots. These guys were ferry pilots with a number "One" priority -- they could bump anybody with a lesser priority, I was one of them. I made the rest of the trip to Chicago and to Des Moines by train. I was home again with the same intent -- to be with my family. No WACs.

While at NAS North Island in San Diego waiting assignment to a squadron, we were again assigned to photo reconnaissance school. This consisted mostly of just horsing around, flying a F6F and taking strip photographs from the Mexican boarder to Laguna Beach. On one such trip I was to make a run at 30,000 feet. It took an hour to reach this altitude. I admit that I wasn't pushing the plane but at the high altitudes I was using full throttle.

When I would reach one end of the run I would make a 180 degree turn and the plane would mush and I would lose 2000 feet. On the run to the other end I would gain 3000 feet. I eventually make it. I was surprised to find that the outside air temperature was 40 degrees below zero and this was the middle of July. Inside the cockpit the temperature was perfectly comfortable even without the cockpit heater. I attributed it to the engine heat on the other side of the fire wall.

It was here at North Island that I was to run into the second of the three guys that I had grown up with. This was Don Preston who was a member of our teenage "gang". Actually, not a gang as we know of them today but a bunch of teenage kids who gathered in Drake Park for playing football, baseball and other sports. We met on the street at the air station and immediately recognized each other even though neither us knew the

other was anywhere near. As it turned out he was an enlisted man and

quartered in another part of the station. Our paths did not cross again. A

few days later I was gone.

11

AUGUST 13, 1944 -- SEPTEMBER 1, 1944
ASSIGNMENT TO SQUADRON VC-93
NAS NORTH BEND, OR

Sometime early in August, I received orders to proceed to North Bend,

Oregon to join Composite Squadron 93, known as VC-93. This trip was

again by train and took about three days to get there. At least I had a

bunk all to myself. On the same train were Bates and Glista. Bates was

going to VC-91 at Astoria and Glista was going to VC-94 at Klamath Falls,

Oregon. Also, on this same train was another pilot (a TBF photo pilot, who

had been in the class after me at Harrisburg), going to the same squadron

that I was headed for, VC-93. This guy's name was James Mallard Wells.

On the train, he came looking for me as I was the other photo

reconnaissance pilot going to NAS North Bend. From that time until the day VC-93 was decommissioned he would be the closest friend I would

have in the squadron. Wells and I departed the train in some small town

in the center of Oregon with about a three hour layover time in this burg

waiting for a bus. Wells decided we should go horseback riding. We found

a stable, rented a couple of "tame" horses and took off over hill and dale.

Ensign James M. Wells

We were riding across somebody's pasture and into somebody's backyard

when we looked up and saw this woman sitting on her back porch. "Ole"

gutsy Wells rides right up to her and strikes up a conversation like he had

known her all his life. She invited us up and we spent about an hour in idle talk while she served us lemonade and cookies. I was beginning to know a very unusual guy.

Just before we boarded the bus we took off for a market where we loaded up on apples, oranges and a few other bits of junk food for the next few hours that we would be spending on the bus. Naturally, we were the last ones on the bus and wound up sitting in the stair well in the entry way of the bus. Wasn't bad! We had a nice little party going before a couple of seats opened up and we had to move.

We arrived at the air station in the very late evening, well after dark, checked in with the duty officer and were told to find our selves a bunk in the junior officer's quarters and come back in the morning. There wasn't anyone in the lobby so we went in the bunk room and in the dark selected a bunk that appeared not to have been claimed by anyone and didn't have a body in it. I was lucky. I guessed right. Wells guessed wrong. Some time later in the middle of the night someone asked him nicely and politely to move.

The following morning we were signed into the squadron and began our training as a member of an organized combat team that we would be with for the next year through thick and thin.

Composite Squadron-93 had been commissioned in February of 1944 at NAS Sandpoint in Seattle, Washington and had spent some time at Astoria, Oregon before coming to North Bend. The squadron's flying personnel had diminished due to deaths, sickness, incompatibility and maybe other reasons. Wells and I were the first replacement pilots to join the squadron. Others were soon to follow and the squadron would continue to receive replacement pilots for various reasons until near the end of our tour with VC-93.

The squadron consisted of twenty four fighter pilots and eighteen bomber pilots. The fighter pilots were divided in to two wings; each wing consisted of three divisions of four planes each. Each division consisted of two sections and each section consisted of two planes. I became the wing man in the second section of the 1st division of the 1st wing. The leader of the 1st wing was the commander of the squadron, Lieutenant Commander Chester Pond Smith. The skipper was also the leader of the 1st division. The 2nd wing was lead by the future executive officer of the squadron, Lieutenant Ira "Redhorse" Myers.

Commander Smith was an engineering graduate of Georgia Tech University and became a naval aviator in 1935. This was his first command. Lieutenant Myers became the executive officer in November when the existing executive officer, a TBM pilot, failed to qualify aboard a carrier. I don't know where Redhorse got his nickname but I suspect that it was from the fact that he was six foot, five inches tall and weighed 256 pounds and was redheaded. He was so big that he had to lower the seat in the plane to the bottom and still duck his head to close the canopy. He was a true "Texan". Prior to joining the squadron he had been an instructor in primary flight school and his most famous student was the actor, Robert Taylor. He was given a gold four-leaf clover medallion by Robert Taylor and his wife Barbara Stanwyck when Taylor graduated from primary flight training.

My first day with the squadron consisted of introductions to the other members of the group, familiarization with the airplane and a check ride with CAG (commander of the air group), Commander Smith. First thing was that I would no longer be flying the F6F but would be flying the FM-2. The FM-2 was still the F4F but had been improved with a 1500 HP engine. Everything else was basically the same and still very comfortable to fly.

On this check ride I was to fly on the skipper's wing through out the whole flight regardless of what he did, loops, rolls, and whatever and not to lose that position. I'm happy to say that he couldn't shake me and I like to think that he was impressed with my flying and that is why I wound up in his division. Actually, I was wing man to "Bugs" Dunagan, the second section leader. We were to fly together for the most part until near the end of our combat tour.

"Bugs" Dunagan had been a seaman and was at Pearl Harbor when it was attacked by the Japanese. He was wounded and had received the Purple Heart. He was chosen by the Navy for flight school and had been a pilot for only a couple of months before I graduated from flight school. I was to remain his wing man until June of 1945 when he took over the lead of the 1st division and I became the section leader in his flight.

We were to remain at North Bend for two weeks before moving on to our next station. During this period we performed the usual combat tactics minus the photo reconn flights. As a matter of fact, I never flew another photographing flight while I was in the Navy. Explain later!

Lt. (j.g.) Willis (Bugs) Dunagan, Lt. (j.g.) Albert (Little Al) Godfrey,
Commander Chester (Skipper) Pond Smith, Ensign Robert Allison

Without a doubt one of the most instructive flights I had occurred here at

North Bend. On this flight, a gunnery target practice flight with Redhorse

Myers, I wasn't causing much damage to the target so Redhorse told me

to pull my plane up beside the target, stay there and watch the tracer

bullets as he made a run. This was to show how far apart the tracers

would be if you let the pipper in the gun sight slide down the rope and

through the target as he made an over head run. As I watched I could see

a tracer pass ahead and the next pass behind. Neither hit the target. Even

if one hit the other would miss. Then he told me to watch while he made

the same over head run and pull back hard on the stick holding the pipper

on the 90 mil ring in the gun sight. A great percentage of the tracers

passed right through the target area. I was then given the chance to try out what I had seen. I could see my own tracers go into the target area. On examination of the target after the flight revealed a good percentage of hits. From that day on I was second only to another lieutenant for high score in the squadron. Also, I indirectly got my butt chewed for holding down on the trigger too long thus supplying a quantity of tracers close to the tow plane. Fortunately, the tow pilot did not know who had made the pass. Nor did I tell him.

In this short period of time at North Bend all the single officers made an over night camping trip to Loon Lake for fishing and a few of the guys went deer hunting with a rifle, a pickup truck and a spot light. Even though they could see the shining eyes of the deer and shot at them from the truck, they didn't score one kill. No fish either. We had to sleep on the ground in our clothes and only one blanket. Even though it was late August it was cold on that mountain. I was never crazy about camping even as a boy scout and this experience didn't improve my attitude toward the outdoor life one bit.

A few days before we were to leave North Bend, Jim Wells was operated on for appendicitis and spent the last few days in the hospital. On the next to last day all the planes at North Bend were to be flown to Sand Point.

This was quite a blow to Wells because it had been his plan to fly one of the TBMs and go visit the wife of Admiral Taffenger, the commandant of the 13th Naval District at Sand Point. He tried to get me to make his social call. I wouldn't have any part of it. First, because I didn't know how well, or if, he knew them. And second, I wasn't socially inclined and could not imagine holding a conversation with the Admiral's wife let a lone the Admiral if he were home. Come to learn that Wells did know the Admiral and his wife as well as their daughter whom he had dated in Washington, D.C. before the war. Upon our return to North Bend the squadron boarded a train and we were off to NAS Holtville at Holtville, CA, Wells included.

12

SEPTEMBER 1, 1944 -- SEPTEMBER 30, 1944
COMBAT FLIGHT TRAINING
NAS HOLTVILLE, CA

The squadron arrived at the air station which is on the edge of the desert about noon. The temperature was well in excess of 100 degrees. Our squadron doctor, Lieutenant Leon Starr, advised the group to be sure to take salt tablets regularly. About five minutes later, at the drinking fountain in the barracks I downed two of these tablets with a swallow of water. I barely made it the head (toilet) before the tablets hit the bottom of my stomach and I was heaving my guts out. I never took another salt tablet after that.

To say it was hot there does not begin to describe the situation. For a hint as to how hot it was, it was necessary to wear gloves and have all your skin covered to be able to crawl into the cockpit of a plane. To have been a mechanic and worked on those planes in the middle of the day must have been plain murder. One consoling factor in flying a plane in that kind heat was that after the plane had climbed to about 5000 feet of altitude you would pass through a level where the air turned from hot to a very comfortable cool.

Holtville was just another extension of the same routine. Included in this routine was quite a bit more night flying where we lost a fighter pilot when he took off from the field and crashed in the All-American canal. He was in the canal all night and was found the next morning. Never discovered what had happened.

Also included was more gunnery practice. On one flight I was assigned as the tow pilot. After the flight had taken off I was to taxi to the end of the runway, wait for a crew to hook on the tow rope, get the signal to go, hold the brakes until I had full throttle, release the brakes, get the tail up and all the speed I could muster, make an eight hundred foot run down the rope, haul back on the stick and pop the plane to about 50 feet of altitude, level off to gain more speed, then fly out to meet the flight so they could make their gunnery runs. Every thing went along normally until

I had the 50 feet of altitude then the engine quit for a few seconds. Before the engine kicked in again the plane had lost most of its altitude and the target, which had popped into the air when it reached the end of the rope, was now dragging through the sage brush. I lost the target returned, landed, taxied around to the end of the runway and did the whole procedure over only to have exactly the same thing happen. This time I returned to the flight line changed to another plane and back again for another target. This time everything went along as it was suppose to. Arriving at the gunnery range I met the flight and with an irritated skipper they began their runs. Each of the twelve planes made a high side pass and then I made a 360 degree turn, while they were gaining altitude for their second run. When I was again flying straight and level, I felt something hit my left leg. I glanced to the left side of the cockpit and noticed the left side of the canopy bobbing up and down. Then I saw that the safety pin was missing. It had somehow become unsnapped and worked its way out. This pin and one on the right side are installed to be pulled to jettison the canopy in case of emergency. I grabbed the edge of the canopy and held it in place with my left hand. The pin had dropped to the bottom of the plane and was not retrievable. So there I sat debating how to handle the situation in that I would have to free up my left hand to be able to lower the wheels and jockey the throttle for landing. I reasoned that if I were to push the canopy fully closed (it had been locked in a position so that it was about two inches open up to this time) that the air rushing over the out side would create a vacuum inside (kind of like the "venturi" effect) and I would be able to use my left hand to handle the plane. So I grabbed the lock lever and shoved the canopy forward. In that instant the wind grabbed the canopy, picked up the left side and slammed it down over my head and around my neck. I was not injured and there I sat, flying straight and level while the flight continued making their gunnery runs. Unfortunately for them, one of them shot the target off during his second run.

The flight rendezvoused and flew back to the field leaving me to my own devises. They weren't aware of my predicament. I headed back to the field. On the way I decided that I didn't want to land with that canopy around my neck so I decided to jettison it all the way. I pulled the other safety pin, ducked and shoved straight up on canopy. It took off, smacked the fuselage right behind my head tearing a large hole in the side of the plane.

The twisted canopy continued down the side of the plane striking the horizontal stabilizer and imbedding itself in the left elevator where it remained for the rest of the ride to the field.

All was not through! After sitting the plane on the runway I began the long taxi back to the flight line. There were three runways that form a triangle and it was necessary to taxi back to the line on two of them, almost always in a heavy cross wind. This required using the brakes to keep the plane on the runway. After a long, tough taxi I arrived at the parking area only to have a gust of wind grab the plane causing the left wing to lift and pull the left wheel off the ground causing a "ground loop" that I couldn't stop. The tip of the right wing was torn up. I would say that that day was a day to forget. The only good thing about it was that I wasn't killed. In view of this "tale of woe", the skipper didn't have the heart to rake me over the coals. In my opinion he didn't have "just" cause.

Every pilot has troubles whether they are his fault or not. For instance, Jim Wells by this time had become known as quite a character. He had gained the reputation of being an individualist. Fact was, Wells was hard of hearing in his left ear and claimed to me that he had been that way since childhood. He had bluffed his way into the cadet program, bluffed his way through the program, and was trying to bluff his way through his time in the squadron without anyone learning of the problem. Since he was in such close proximity to the skipper of the TBMs and the squadron doctor they began to suspect the handicap because he was always the "bird who didn't get the word". The two of them, when talking to Wells, would put their hands in front of their mouths just to confuse him. Half his hearing came from being able to read lips. Even though he should have been taken off flight duty, the problem hadn't caused any serious problems in flying. They had no intentions of causing him any further trouble.

The only problem I can recall was the time the TBMs were to make bombing runs on a target in the Salton Sea. The planes were to make runs from north to south starting at 10,000 feet and pulling out at 1500. Everybody complied except Wells. He reasoned because of the wind direction, the best run could be made from east to west and pulling out a little lower. He did with the result that he was flying right through the paths of the bomb drops of the other planes. The air waves were blue from the leader of the flight. Wells would provide a source of comment and humor for the rest of our tour.

Probably the most humorous thing that took place for the group while we were at Holtville was an outing of the squadron officers and the spouses of the married officers. The whole group journeyed to Mexicali, Mexico, just across the border from Calexico, CA, to take in a bull fight. After the Gringos witnessed a few sessions with the bulls, they become bored and restless. To liven things up, the skipper volunteered to ride the bull while the Matador stuck it. The skipper was so far gone on booze he could hardly walk but he made it to the railing and promptly fell on his face into the arena. The security guards pushed him back in the stands. He bowed to applause of the Gringos but was the subject of scorn by the Mexican fans. Never the less, during the next event he was back, flat on his face again in the arena. This time the security escorted him all the way out. At the end of the festivities, the gang went looking for him and found him outside the gates to where the dead bulls are dragged from the arena. He was down on his hands and knees with a bunch of poor Mexicans trying to cut a steak from a dead bull with his pocket knife. His wife was furious. Conduct unbecoming an officer, well, maybe so, but you would never convince the officers of that squadron he was guilty of bad conduct. It was one of the most memorable fun days we were to have. In fact, the skipper was probably the best squadron commander in the Navy. He was a gentleman and a truly compassionate man, even when he had a little too much to drink on too many occasions.

Seems like everywhere you go there is always some guy who has to shoo the females off like they were flies. Ninety nine percent of the men have to work their butts off just to be even glanced at. Then there was the Roy Kinnard type of guy. Roy was tall, blonde, well built and good looking, who, when he enter a room or bar all female eyes just gravitated to him and many of the girls left their companions to make a play for him. He truly did shoo them off. He would actually be bored and even annoyed with them. It pissed most of the rest of us no end. We ugly guys were used to being ignored.

Another aspect of our training was the "Delbert Dunker". This was a contraption that was constructed to resemble the cockpit of a plane. We were each required to strap ourselves into the seat. The Dunker was lifted to about 10 feet high over the swimming pool and dropped in the deep-end of the pool. Now you are under water. You can't see any thing and you are expected to unhook yourself and get out before you drown. There are instructors there to make sure you don't drown. The object of this exercise is to become familiar with a water landing and possibly save someone from panicking in the event of the real thing. Little would I know that I would have a first hand experience with the real McCoy, not once but twice.

While at Holtville, the skipper would have trouble with one of the enlisted men, a black steward's mate whom I had encountered in North Bend. He was quite a pleasant, friendly guy at North Bend. I would never have expected trouble with him. Wouldn't you know his last name was Friend. His home was in Los Angeles and as we passed through LA on our way to Holtville he jumped the train. Was picked up by the shore patrol and given a reprimand. A couple of weeks after arriving at Holtville, he decided that he and the rest of the blacks were not going to be segregated in the mess hall. They were challenged by the whites and a riot ensued. Friend was court-marshaled and placed in the Marine brig in El Central, CA. The report was that the marine guards nearly beat him to death. Too bad for "ole" Friend! He just lived before his time!

The squadron had been commissioned with 37 officers and 134 enlisted men. Before we were to leave Holtville for NAS Los Alamitos at Long Beach, California, the squadron was streamlined into a Composite squadron consisting of only flying officers and flying crewmen and about five administrative officers and a hand full of key ground enlisted men. The rest were released to the local CASU unit at Holtville for reassignment.

13

OCTOBER 1, 1944 -- DECEMBER 1, 1944 FLIGHT TRAINING, CARRIER OPERATIONAL TRAINING, NAS LOS ALAMITOS, CA

The arrival on October 1st at Los Alamitos was to begin a pre-departure training period. This was to consist of simulated strikes, field carrier landing and formation tactics. The bomber squadron was sent to San Diego for anti submarine warfare training. Also included in our program was carrier qualification aboard the USS Matanikau, CVE 101. It was from the Matanikau that Ensign Robert Reed made a high and fast approach for a landing and sailed over the barrier, ran off the forward end of the flight deck, and dumped his plane in the ocean ahead of the ship. He escaped the disaster unharmed and fortunately did not have his crew with him. No harm, no foul, just embarrassment.

Some of the older members of the squadron had not been subjected to carrier landings in combat type planes and were about to make their first. Most did OK, but our executive officer Lieutenant Occo Gibbs could not bring himself to land aboard the carrier. He was disqualified for carrier operations by the Captain of the Matanikau and was released from the squadron. Occo was an OS2U observation plane pilot and had always been catapulted from a cruiser and landed on the water prior to coming to the squadron. He just couldn't get the nerve to come aboard the carrier. Might not have been nerves so much as just plain smart. He had to fly back and land at San Diego.

The new executive officer of the squadron was to be Redhorse and Lieutenant William " Mule" Skinner was to become the commander of the bomber group.

Los Alamitos is near Seal Beach, CA and just east of Long Beach. The inclement weather gave the members of the squadron a sizable amount of liberty. We would wake up in the morning, look out the window, see the fog or rain, call the flight line to find that flying had been canceled then get an early start for Long Beach or Los Angeles. These nasty mornings were called "Crapo secure us", a play of words on the various cloud formations. Results-- more sack time!

So it was on one of these days that another pilot, Charlie Janson, and I took off for Long Beach. I have no idea what we had in mind for that day, but what ever it was, we stopped in a restaurant on Ocean Boulevard, sat down at the counter and lo and behold my future was sitting at the other end. She was with another female which made it just right for making a pass. I believe it was Charlie who had the glib tongue and made the first move. It was the beginning of a pair of very nice friendships for Charlie and me. Not only were they nice looking, but friendly and they had a car. In the two months that we were stationed at Los Alamitos, Charlie and his lady friend, Wilda, with my future and me spent several very enjoyable days and evenings in and around Long Beach and Los Angeles. My female interest, Margie, and Wilda had been student nurses and roommates at Los Angeles General Hospital. Margie still worked there. The four of us remained close friends until Charlie and I sailed away. I continued to correspond with Margie all the time we were at sea. I don't know if Charlie and Wilda had any contact during this time but theirs was not to be a lasting affair, anyhow. Charlie was killed a few months later. I'll get back to Margie and me later.

Robert Allison, Margie Wada, Wilda Van Pelt, Charles Janson

While at Los Alamitos the USO presented a program featuring Bing Crosby and Bob Hope. This was without a doubt the number one attraction of all USO shows along with a few "Big Bands". It was rumored that the reason Los Alamitos got the show was because it was so near Hollywood and the station chaplain, a Catholic priest, was a friend of Crosby's. Stands to reason!

You can believe that we were more than eager to see them. It was like the young people today seeing the Beatles, Rolling Stones, or Elvis in their prime. But it was not to be! It was a couple of days before the show that the squadron received orders to report to the USS Matanikau. So we spent the evening of the show listening to their broadcast on radio on board the ship and griping all the while.

If there had been any vindication for us it was because Crosby, Hope and the Chaplain refused to begin the show until a large section of the seats in center and down front that had been set aside for senior officers and their spouses or lady friends had been cleared of these civilians and replaced with service men. The high ranking officers and their friends left. If you had ever been confronted with "RHIP" (Rank has its privileges) as existed in the service you can well imagine what this did to the morale of the sailors. You can well imagine the political influence Crosby and Hope carried to be able to attack the brass in their own lair.

Toward the end of our stay at Los Alamitos the squadron held a party at the Pacific Coast Club in Long Beach. Due to the presence of some of the wives of the married officers the party didn't get too much out of hand although a large quantity of hard liquor was consumed. At least the bill for the booze was six hundred dollars which, at that time, was a considerable amount of liquor. But, we had our drunks and my friend Wells was one of them. He spent most of the evening with his head hanging in the toilet with me holding him up so that he wouldn't drown in his own puke. Don't remember how we got back to the station. I'm sure we had Skinner and the doctor to thank for it.

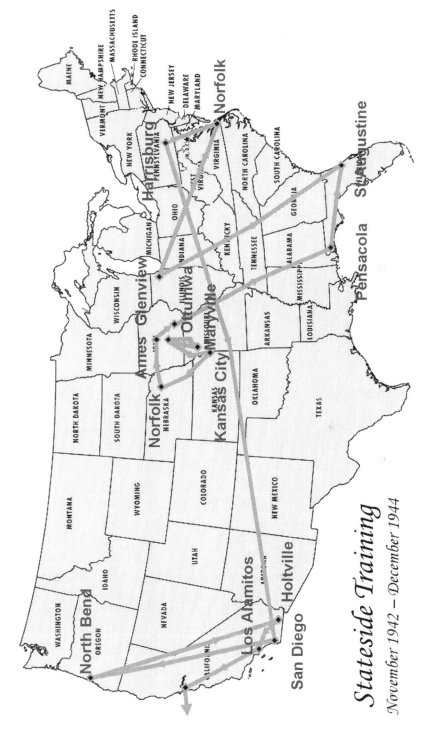

Stateside Training
November 1942 – December 1944

14

DECEMBER 1, 1944 -- DECEMBER 26, 1944
EMBARCATION TO OAHU, HI
NAS KANEOHE

On the third of December, 1944, the squadron was packed up and packed

off to San Diego and loaded aboard the USS Shamrock Bay, CVE-88, for a

cruise to Pearl Harbor. During this five day cruise we were accompanied

by another VC squadron. The Shamrock Bay was serving as a transport for

planes and personnel on its way to the south pacific where it would pick

up the squadron, VC-94, and Walt Glista. There were so many passengers

there weren't rooms for everyone so we were stowed everywhere. My

cot was in the after windy passage. That is a very narrow hall way from

one side the ship to the other just under the flight deck and above the

hangar deck. Was bad enough but we also were blessed with one of our group, who came aboard in slightly more than a drunken condition, that wasn't helped by the motion of the sea. Needless to say, to our discomfort, he was heaving his guts out day and night for three days.

On the way to Pearl Harbor, we circled by San Francisco where we were joined by the battleship, USS Texas, and her escort. Beings the Shamrock Bay was ferrying passengers and planes to the south pacific, the deck was filled with planes and no flights were possible from the carrier. So I guess we were being protected by the Texas. One interesting thing about the trip was that the Texas had gunnery practice with her 16 inch guns. We watched from the flight deck and we could actually see the 16 inch projectiles flying through the air.

After arriving at Pearl Harbor, we were transported across the island to NAS Kaneohe. I don't remember my thoughts when we entered Pearl Harbor. I don't even remember seeing the USS Arizona. I'm sure I must have had some deep emotions about the place because of my brother having been there during the attack on December 7, 1941.

All that Honolulu meant to me at this time was a place for liberty. This we did on several occasions. All I can remember of the town was Trader Vic's bar and the Royal Hawaiian Hotel. At Kaneohe, the only entertainment was the beach and baseball. The squadron did arrange for a "native luau". This was held jointly for the enlisted men and the officers. It had all the trimmings: barbecued pig, coconuts and hula girls. One of the hula girls wiggled her fanny in the face of one of the aircrew men sitting next to the dance floor, and pulled him to his feet to dance with her. The front of his shorts showed where his mind was. He got good laugh and a big round of applause.

Part of our training while at Kaneohe was another practice session of carrier landings, this time on the USS Bataan, CVE-29. Each of us made eight landings except for Ensign Malcolm Williams, who dumped his TBM in the water and Ensign Ike Scherer went over the starboard bow. Ike struck his head and received a few cuts on his noggin. He was picked up by a destroyer but had no recollection of the accident.

As I returned from my turn at practice landings, my flight flew over the Pearl Harbor anchorage. While passing over I looked down and could see a ship that appeared to be a battleship of the USS South Dakota class. I had no idea my brother, Melv, was in Pearl Harbor at the time. As far as I knew he was somewhere in the South Pacific. After landing at Kaneohe, Jim Wells and I took off over the Pali by bus for Pearl Harbor. Upon arriving at the fleet landing we could see the ship tied up at Ford Island and sure enough, it was the Indiana. We caught the shore boat at the fleet landing and went out to the ship, went aboard, told the duty officer that we wanted to see my brother, Chief Yeoman Melvin Allison. He called for a messenger and had the messenger take us down to the navigation office. When we got there a 1st class yeoman told us that Melv had gone over the Pali to see me at Kaneohe and if we were to show up on the Indiana to hold us there until he got back. We had passed each other as we crossed the Pali. We waited and he got back later in the evening. The reason he knew that I was in Hawaii was because he had just returned from Bremerton, WA where he had been able to visit with our parents. My mother had told him I was at Kaneohe. We spent the rest of the evening with him until it was so late that we couldn't make it back to Kaneohe before curfew. So we spent the night in the chief's quarters. The next morning we were treated to a first class tour of the Indiana by Melv, even to getting into the breech mechanism of the sixteen inch guns. Melv, who had the responsibility of assigning "General Quarters" stations for the crew, had assigned himself to the "Fire Control" station. This was on the lower level of the fire control room. These two rooms were oval shaped and had 18 inches of steel all the way around and over head and under foot. It would have taken a sixteen inch shell to have gotten to him.

He was not on the Indiana, a newly commissioned ship, during the attack but was on temporary duty with the Admiral on the USS Dobbin. When the attack started he happened to be ashore. Upon returning to the harbor during the attack, a motor launch put him on the USS Raleigh where he wound up passing ammunition.

A few days later Melv returned to Kaneohe and had three or four other guys that we had gone to school with in Des Moines. They just happened to be in Pearl Harbor at that time. When they departed that day he took with him a carry-all bag containing seven bottles of whiskey, four of which I had brought with me from San Diego and three that I had gotten after arriving at Pearl. I don't know why I did this other than I knew I would be getting more and whiskey wasn't high on my priority list..

On December 24, I made the trip to the Indiana again. This time I declined the assistance of the messenger and proceeded toward the chief's quarters. Going down the passage way I could see a sailor squatting on the deck. When I got there and turned the corner I found Melv and about twenty other chiefs having a Christmas drinking party. There in the middle of the deck sat my "former" seven bottles and quite a few other bottles.

The Indiana had just returned to Pearl from Bremerton with these guys and a lot of smuggled booze. The party had been going on some time because some of these guys were well on their way to being smashed. I spent the night there and returned to Kaneohe Christmas day. I had to be back to pack my gear because the squadron was returning to Pearl Harbor that night to go aboard the USS Long Island, CVE-1. We were departing the morning of December 26th for the long voyage to The Admiralty Islands.

I planned on being up early the next morning and out on deck in hopes of seeing and waving at Melv as the Long Island pulled out from astern of the Indiana and passed by her on our way to the open sea. The next morning I awoke to the rolling of the ship, dashed out on the deck and found myself several miles outside the harbor. I had slept through the whole operation.

15

DECEMBER 26, 1944 -- JANUARY 8, 1945 TRANSPORTATION TO PITILU, MANUS, ADMIRALTY ISLANDS

The USS Long Island had been an oil tanker. But at the request of the Navy, it was converted into an escort carrier for antisubmarine duty. There was also an order for the construction of several more escort carriers for submarine duty and for the direct support of Army and Marine landing forces. The main contractor for these ships was a guy named Henry J. Kaiser. The CVE's were to be nick-named "Kaiser Coffins". The main reason for this was the one quarter inch steel plate that was the skin of the ship. This skin sprung back and forth in heavy seas making eerie, booming noises. The name also came from the fact that if hit by a torpedo you couldn't get off fast enough.

The Long Island had become a transport ship and the accommodations for the "transportees" were what had once been bulk oil tanks. They were now our living quarters with a mob of bunks stacked five high. You can well imagine the heat and the smell as we traveled across the equator. More men slept on the flight deck than those who slept in bunks.

The high light of this cruise was the "ordeal" of the "Royal Order of the Deep". This initiation was the process of a "Pollywog" becoming a "Shellback". In the case of this ferry, there were so many Pollywogs that we had to line up and run through the process as quickly as possible. It might have been quick but it didn't lose any of the brutality that had been its reputation.

First you were forced to lie down on your stomach in a gutter of salt water and endure a bunch of sadistic A-holes strapping you across the butt with strips of canvas about two feet long soaked in salt water. From there, you were herded into the royal court where you were obligated to kneel before the "Royal Bar", a metal rod that you had to grip with both hands and received a jolt of electricity that shook our eye teeth. Next, we had bow to King Neptune and his queen and then kiss the big fat belly of a big fat chief dressed in a diaper. This slob was the "Royal Baby".

From there you were forced to sit on a straight backed chair with its back to the "Royal" swimming pool. While you were sitting there your mouth was stuffed with water, soap suds and turpentine and then you were pushed over backward into the pool. The pool was about 20 feet square with at least ten "Royal" polar bears in it. It was their job to keep you under the water until you reached the other side. I went under on the first shove and didn't you come up until I was crawling up the other side on my way out. Once over the side and on the deck you were forced to run about fifty feet through a gauntlet of sailors with these canvas straps whacking you across your posterior until you could climb over a ten foot cargo net.

Once you were over, you were a Shellback, never to suffer this "bullshit" again. But it gave you the authority to inflict these indignities on other Pollywogs crossing the equator. This I was able to do many years later, but not so violently, on my wife and others on a cruise ship out of Rio. If you think I was kidding about the extent of energy expended by these sailors, let me assure you my behind and every other Pollywog's butt was black and blue for days. One Pollywog, trying to be cute, put a couple of oranges in his tee shirt before starting this initiation. His cuteness invited considerably more attention from the sadists than was imposed on the rest of us. He wound up in sick bay.

The most interesting thing that occurred on this "cruise" was that we went to bed on December 31, 1944 and woke up the next morning, January 2, 1945. We had crossed the International Date Line during the night. We missed the whole day of January 1st. But, we were to regain the lost day when we re-crossed the International Date Line on the way back in July, living the same day twice as we returned to Hawaii and home. Unfortunately, these two days were spent at sea with nothing to see but the horizon.

16

JANUARY 8, 1945 -- FEBRUARY 11, 1945
NAS PITYILU

The trip to the Admiralties took from the 26th of December, 1944 to the

7th of January, 1945, minus the lost day on 1/1/45. The Admiralty Islands

are three degrees below the equator and about 120 degrees above zero

degrees Fahrenheit. Sure as hell didn't need my winter flight gear there.

The ship dropped anchor in Seadler Harbor, Manus, Admiralty Islands. Our

squadron was to have relieved VC-76. We were late and they had left a

couple of days earlier for the Linguyan operation, supposedly our

operation.

The squadron and its equipment were transported by LCI to Pitilu, a small

island on the outer reef of the harbor. This island contained one airstrip

made of crushed coral and the living area for the squadron and about

5,000 thousand other sailors. The living quarters were Quonset huts that held about 20 men. These were corrugated metal huts constructed in a grove of coconut palms so it was necessary to be careful where you were walking. One coconut on the head was a trip in a body bag. It was not uncommon in the middle of the night to have a coconut drop on the Quonset hut, ring out like the "Bell's of St. Mary" and shake the hell out of that tin can.

The head (restroom) was a covered hut at the end of a dock built out over the water inside the reef. The sides were laced with strips of olive colored cloth that gave a feeling of no privacy. The showers were out in the open and there was usually a string of naked men walking down the street with a towel over their shoulder. One day, as we were walking down the street, two jeeps loaded with nurses from a hospital ship drove down the same street. As you might guess no one made an effort to cover up. I guess you might say that we could have been the first "streakers". And I guess you might say that the nurses didn't show any signs of being impressed. At least I didn't hear any "oohs and ahs".

We were cautioned upon arrival in these islands about the disease called Malaria. It is a disease that is spread by mosquitoes and is something that will lay you low with fever, headaches and diarrhea and make you shake like a dog passing razor blades and make you wish you were dead. To prevent this disease we were ordered to take Atabrine. These were little yellow tablets taken orally with water. The pills would turn a person's skin as yellow as the color of the pills had been before he had taken them. There were a lot of yellow people on that little bitty island.

We had pretty much the same flying routine with the addition of simulated attacks on ships. The one I can remember was making practice runs on was a British cruiser. Regardless of how brave I thought I was at the time, I'm glad that it wasn't a Japanese cruiser. That would have been a situation we would have been in if it hadn't been for the "fickle finger of fate". If our squadron had been on a training schedule three months earlier, we may have very well been on board the Petrof Bay or one of the other CVE's, of which some didn't "fair so well", in October and been involved in the Lye Gulf operation. We would have been involved in a very serious battle with the Japanese fleet in the Gulf in place of VC-76, the squadron that we were scheduled to relieve on January 7th. This was the last battle that VC 76 was supposed to have been subjected to. The battle was fought between a task force of Japanese battleships and a task force of gutsy brave American "Escort Carriers" and destroyers. Against overwhelming odds, the "Escort Carriers" and destroyers won the battle due to timidity of the Japanese Admiral, who believed that an American task force of large carriers and battleships was near by. He was wrong. Halsey and the fast fleet weren't within hundreds of miles. The Japanese could have wiped out the escort carriers and demolished the American invasion forces, leaving a mass of sunken American ship and thousands of dead and wounded in Leyte Gulf. The planes and the destroyers of the escort carrier task force gave the Japanese hell and were largely responsible for the defense of the landing party. And as the "fickle finger of fate" would have it VC 76 was to receive two more operations, Linguyan and Iwo Jima that were scheduled for VC-93. Was it their "bad luck" or our "good luck", maybe? I would have liked to have been in those two operations. Not only had the person in charge of scheduling ships missed the "boat", he had caused our squadron to miss the "boat".

As I was saying, the airfield consisted of one strip of white coral. The high heat reflecting off the coral gave an extra lift to the plane while over the runway on takeoff. When the plane passed over the hot, white sandy beach and over the cooler air of the dark water the extra lift disappeared and causing the plane to mush because of a lack of airspeed giving the feel of settling into the water. A God awful eerie feeling when you can do nothing about it but wait!

It was on this Island that Jim Wells' true personality really began to reveal itself. Due to the number of people on the island, transportation was at a premium. The squadron was assigned one jeep for the skipper and one personnel carrier for the rest of us. Anywhere you went was on foot. This included walking down to the flight line. You can imagine our surprise when here comes Wells driving up to the barracks in an eight wheel truck. He had conned the transportation officer out of the thing with the story of how he needed transportation for his photographic work. Since it was the only vehicle available, he took it. I don't think he took a picture while he was on the island. However, he did gain access to their photo lab where he helped himself to their photographs. Don't know why he needed the truck, he didn't have anywhere to go.

Not only was the truck in his name, but he wouldn't let anyone else use it. The truck had a right hand drive since we were on a British island and we were required to drive on the left side of the streets, which is strange since everyone on the island was an American. A truck wasn't his only possession, but he claims to have taken possession of a F6F fighter plane that had been surveyed (that is: written off the books by the Navy). While he was there, he increased his supply of government issued gear. Normally each officer had one cruise box for all his gear including uniforms, Wells had three and gaining on four. He had extra of everything, not just one extra but six or more of everything. If he could have gotten that stuff home he could have opened a war surplus store after the war. I do have to say he was pretty generous to the rest of us when we needed a pair of gloves or anything he had.

Swimming and searching for shells on the reef was one of the main sources of recreation. There were several of the men who constructed sailboats out of various pieces of junk found around the base. One of the favorite pieces of junk was abandoned drop-able gas tanks. One fine day, Roy Kinnard and I confiscated one of these "tank" sailboats and put to sea. That is, at sea inside the reef. For the most part the water is shallow but in places it gets over your head. Well, neither of us had every sailed a sailboat in our lives and we immediately capsized the thing in water over our heads. We worked for hours swimming and dragging that can against a light current until we got it beached about a mile from where we had departed. The mast and sails were mutilated mass. We abandoned the thing there and "thank God" we never heard from the owner.

17

FEBRUARY 11, -- MARCH 10, 1945
TRANSPORTATION TO NAS AGANA, GUAM

The Linguyan operation had been completed and the fleet was returning to the Ulithi anchorage. We were put on the USS Barnes, CVE -20, for transportation to Ulithi where we would, at last, relieve VC-76 on board the USS Petrof Bay, CVE-80. We arrived at Ulithi anchorage only to find that the Petrof Bay and VC-76 had left the day before for the Iwo Jima operation. We had missed again. Since we could not get aboard the Petrof Bay we stayed aboard the Barnes and traveled on to NAS Agana on the island of Guam.

We were to remain at Agana for three weeks at the end of which time the Petrof Bay returned to Guam and we relieved VC-76. During our time at Agana we continued the usual training routines and spent a couple of days on the USS Thetis Bay, CVE-90, where we made a few more practice landings. Practice landings are like practice parachute jumps, each one is the real thing, it's either successful or it isn't. The idea of practice landings is to develop your technique so that under less ideal combat conditions things might be a little less "hairy".

For composite squadrons aboard CVE's we had only FM-2s to fly. On Guam there was a shortage of FMs so we had to do our flying in F6Fs and F4Us. I had quite a bit of experience in the F6F and none in the F4U so here was my chance to check out in this fancy, good looking, inverted gull winged plane that was considered one of the best fighter planes in the world. One morning Al Godfrey and I, each, checked out an F4U and after taking a few minutes to check out the cockpit and familiarize ourselves with the controls and instruments, we climbed in, started the engines and taxied to the end of the runway. We both pulled on to the runway with me on Godfrey's wing. This was mistake number one. We should not have taken off in formation. The usual procedure for a formation takeoff is for the lead pilot to hold his plane on the runway until the wing man is airborne. This we did but Al did not look back to see if I was airborne and did not speed up his plane. I was holding my plane back at a dangerously slow air speed and concentrating intently on holding my position on Al's plane when I glanced out the opposite side of my plane only to find that the right wing was only about six inches from the ground. It scared the hell out of me. I poured the throttle to my plane and left Al literally sitting on the runway. I have to say that I was shocked to feel the tremendous burst of power that that two thousand horse power engine kicked forth.

After we rendezvoused, we climbed to about 15,000 feet where we were pounced upon from above by a couple of F6Fs. A dog fight ensued and I found myself in a tail chase with one of the F6Fs. I also found, that an F4U was no match with the F6F in turns. I kept drawing my plane tighter and tighter, the next thing I knew the plane snapped on its back and I found myself hurtling for the ocean in a spin. I rolled the plane upright and pulled hard back on the stick and in an instant I was on my back again in a high speed stall. This time I rolled out and very gently eased back on the stick. The plane came out of its dive screaming. I don't think I ever traveled so fast, as a matter of fact I know I hadn't. Anyhow, that was the end of the dog fight. Al and I rendezvoused again and returned to the field. Since NAS Agana strip is located on a hill top about 500 feet above an army air force field, we were required to make right hand landing patterns. I followed Al in and as I leveled out over the end of the runway I held the plane about 15 feet in the air until it stalled. Like any other plane it should have settled down to the runway. It didn't! It stalled and the right wing dropped causing the plane to land on the right wheel, bounced, came down on the left wheel, bounced, and came down on the right wheel. Finally I got the plane down and was home free. That was as much of the F4U as I wanted or needed.

A strange thing happened that afternoon. Another flyer, not from our squadron, checked out an F4U, maybe the same one I had been flying, and took off down the runway. He had apparently forgotten to set the trim tabs on the elevators and because of the power of this plane, it shot almost straight up in the air. The last that was seen of the pilot, he was trying to crawl out of the plane as it stalled, turned on its back and plunged into one of the maintenance hangers.

I had another situation occur a day or so later when I was flying wing on Bugs Dunagan. We were flying FM-2s and practicing the Thatch weave against two others of our group. They came down on us from an over head run. We pulled straight up so quickly and with such force that the plexi-glass in the cockpit canopy popped out of its frame right into the cockpit with me. Gave me quite a start as it took a couple of seconds to figuring out what had happened.

Now that I had flown all three navy fighter planes I feel qualified in comparing them. The F4U was considered to be faster than the F6F but not by much if anything. Both were faster by far than the FM-2 but the FM-2 was considerably more maneuverable than either of the others. I believe, if given the choice of flying one of them in combat I would choose the F6F. But flying from a carrier I would prefer the FM-2. An example of how dependable an FM-2 was is a situation that occurred to Walt Glista on board the USS Shamrock Bay. His FM-2 was sitting on the catapult under full power waiting for the launch mechanism to be fired when the metal ring that holds the anchor on the tail end of the plane broke. The plane in this position is about 70 feet from the leading edge of the flight deck. Without the assistance of the catapult Glista flew that plane off the deck, and literally held it in the air. Its tail wheel was dragging in the water before gathering enough speed to climb. No other combat plane in the world could have accomplished that.

Impossible, you say, to make a fly-away take off with only a seventy foot run! Well, maybe. I, too, had a hard time accepting something I didn't see. So I am considering the possibility of the feat.

First, assuming the plane's wheels are ten feet behind the propeller, the run down the deck would be eighty feet, not seventy. The plane was sitting with brakes released and under it's engine's full 1500 horse power and propeller adjusted to full low pitch, when the holding ring broke releasing the plane. The wind velocity and the forward motion of the ship were creating a flow of air over the wings of twenty one knots before the plane moved an inch. This speed, combined with the pull of the propeller must reach a minimum of sixty three knots to maintain level flight. In addition, as the plane leaves the flight deck it has about forty feet to fall before hitting the water, adding more speed to whatever its speed it had attained at the end of the flight deck, in reaching that sixty three knots. The plane does not fall straight down but continues it's forward motion adding more time until it either hits the water or flies away. Another condition that could help attain the necessary speed is the pitch of the ship. There is always a rise and a fall to the fore and aft line of the ship due to the wave or the swell action. If the ring broke at the moment the ship was at an even keel and is on it's way down stroke of this pitch, then a down hill attitude would exist on the ship and the plane would travel with less resistance making it easier to add speed thus adding to the attained airspeed.

In a normal fly-away takeoff, the first plane in line for takeoff is about three hundred feet from the leading edge of the flight deck and must reach this same sixty three knots. It was quite normal for a FM-2 to be airborne well before this three hundred feet is used up and be several feet in the air when passing over the end of the flight deck indicating that, maybe, only two hundred feet would be used to lift off the deck. So, maybe it's not unreasonable that Glista's plane did cover that eighty-two feet and did fly away I have no reason to doubt the report. As a matter of fact, I believe it!

During this time many of the Marines who were wounded at Iwo Jima were transported to Guam for treatment. Our squadron Doctor, Lt. Starr, was transferred to the naval hospital on Guam to lend a hand with his special talents. This he was happy to do for there wasn't much surgery to practice in our squadron.

One of the things that Wells and I did for amusement while there was to go to the north end of the island to an army camp to go hunting with a squad of these "doggies". The hunt was to be on the cliffs overlooking the ocean where the few remaining Japanese soldiers were hiding. What we were to hunt were these Japs. Unfortunately, or fortunately as the case may be, it was raining on the cliffs and the "doggies" do not go down there in the rain because the rain deadens the sounds and it is too easy to be surprised by the enemy. We spent a little time listening to the tales, true or not true, of these hunts. They might inflate the truth but they had little jars of gold teeth that they had removed from the mouths of the dead (or nearly dead} and other personal items belonging to these dead. I don't think now that I would relish the memory of shooting or even seeing a man shot even if he was the enemy. Shooting a plane out of the sky and killing the pilot seemed not to have been a problem for me nor do I think that I would be bothered by the memory of it now.

The beaches at Guam were first class. The one we used was at the bottom of the cliff at Agana and just beyond the army air force field. This was the beach were the marines had invaded just nine months before. There were still rusted out tanks sitting in the water off shore and in the jungle and hills along the beach there were still concrete pillboxes and other fortifications but in some disrepair from the shelling and flame throwers. We spent quite a bit of time browsing through these fortifications and caves and tunnels looking for souvenirs. After being probably the 10,000th snooper, the only thing we found were a few tattered and burned bits of clothing and a few shoes that were weathered and coming apart and with the bones of the feet still in them.

Several years after the war, I came across a book with a picture of this beach. It had been taken by our squadron photographer of a group of our officers in swimming trunks lounging on the sand with several young women also in swimming suits. I recognized the guys in the picture with the women. The picture was taken on one of our outings. The women were Navy Nurses and Red Cross ladies from NAS Agana. The picture had been selected from the ships photographic files to be printed in a book published after the war.

The name of the book was "Escort Carriers in Action". The book was paid for by Richard Reynolds of the Reynolds Tobacco Company, who was the navigation officer on the USS Makin Island, and a copy was issued to every member of the ship's crew of the escort carriers but not the members of the air groups that flew from them. Strange deal, since the only reason these carriers were out there was because of the pilots and air crewmen.

I often wondered if any of the wives of the married guys in the picture every saw this book and became aware of the fact that their husbands were entertaining other women while they were suppose to be out fighting a war. Actually it was just a chance encounter, not planned by anyone.

Another nutty thing that Wells and I pulled was to take all the duplicate phonograph records that were issued to the squadron to an army camp nearby and trade them for two carbines, a 30 caliber rifle and a bit of ammunition. This was on the "QT" and no one ever found out. I don't know if Wells ever got his rifle home or not but I had traded my carbine off for some thing that escaped my memory long before we got back to the states.

One thing about our housing was that it was Quonset huts again. They sit on the bare ground that was a fine red dust. At night while trying to sleep in the heat we would sweat and the sheets that we slept on became a red mud mat. We only had to sleep on them for a week before getting another set. We did wash them ourselves occasionally.

For the first couple of nights that we were in these huts one of the other ensigns would wake up in the middle of the night having a nightmare and screaming that the Japs were slitting his throat. The stories going around were that there had been a few instances of that happening before we got there and there were still occasional times when a Japanese soldier would get into a chow line because he was hungry.

The second of two USO shows that I was to see was at Agana. This was a daytime show that featured two well known light-heavy weight boxers. One was George Abrams, this I remember because my Uncle's name was Abram. The other's name, I don't remember. They were to put on an exhibition of boxing and the referee was Commander Gene Tunney, a former world heavy-weight champion. After sitting and waiting for about an hour with a throng of sailors for the show to start, here comes a delegation of senior officers escorting the locally stationed nurses and Red Cross women to take their seats at ringside. This "exhibition" wasn't to well received by the throng.

The demonstration was the poorest example of boxing you could ever imagine. The two boxers hung on each other and it's doubtful if they threw a punch. Tunney just stood to the side, leaning on the ropes and did nothing. The hoots and boos became a crescendo. Some sailor yelled out: "You wouldn't be standing there like a dummy if Dempsey were in there, Tunney!" Not too much respect for the uniform, even less for the man.

The boos got so bad the commanding Admiral stood up and told the crowd that if they didn't shut up and stop the noise he would have the whole bunch marched out in double file. Things quieted down but the fight didn't get any better.

The last couple of days that we were on Guam we were sent to the harbor to wait for the Petrof Bay to come in from Iwo Jima. The evening before we were to shove off we went to the officers club there at the harbor. This club was right next to Admiral Nimitz's quarters and his swimming pool. Everything was going along fine until Al Godfrey had to empty his bladder and went into the bushes by the pool and cut loose. He was observed by the Shore Patrol and arrested. Since we were leaving the next morning he was released to the custody of the skipper. Once we were out to sea the captain of the ship received a message from Nimitz's office wanting to know what punishment the skipper had given to Godfrey. The skipper was forced to confine him to quarters for three days which didn't bother Godfrey because we would be at sea for those three days. Thank God, he didn't use the Admiral's swimming pool.

Incidentally, the sand used in the construction of Nimitz's swimming was imported from the Gulf of Mexico to Guam because of its pure white color. This is hear-say but probably true. After seeing the snow white sand on the beach in Cancun years later, while on vacation, I now believe the story.

18

MARCH 10, 1945 -- MARCH 21, 1945
OKINAWA OPERATION

The Petrof Bay had been commissioned in 1944 and had been involved in three invasions with VC-76 aboard before we relieved them. It had been a good ship and VC-76 a good squadron both with fine records which we expected to live up to. The accommodations for the squadron's officers were two and four man staterooms for the lieutenants, a single for the squadron commander and nine man bunk rooms for most of the ensigns. There were a few state rooms for some of the less senior lieutenants and those ensigns that didn't object to being deep in the ship in what we called "torpedo junction". If one of those CVEs took a torpedo, it would practically sink before you could get out of bed. That is, if the torpedo didn't explode in bed with you.

125

The ship was about 500 feet long and the flight deck was about 490 feet and 70 feet wide. The landing area was contained on the after third of the flight deck. For a fly-away take off the forward two thirds of the deck was used. The ship had one catapult for launching planes into the air. This was on the forward left hand corner of the flight deck. The tail end of the plane was snapped to the deck by a metal hook with a breakable metal ring. The forward end of the plane was attached to a wire rope sling to a hook in the deck. This hook was only about 70 feet from the leading end of the flight deck. The hook was fired down the deck by compressed air at a speed of 70 knots. The plane was instantly traveling 70 knots and was thrown off the front end of the flight deck where it was now flying under its own power. It is quite an operation, exciting, a little spooky at first but once fired you are sure you are going to leave to ship. All you need is for that engine to keep running full power.

Life aboard a carrier is quite pleasant for the officers and I would say that it is not bad for the enlisted men either. Certainly, the food is a darned sight better on a large ship than on any small vessel.

On March 10th we departed Guam for Ulithi. As we sailed into the Ulithi anchorage, I was on deck, as I usually was when entering or leaving a harbor. The first thing I saw was ships. Warships, cargo ships, tankers, hospital ships, every kind of ship you could imagine. There were thousands of them. They ranged from carriers and battleships to LCTs and PT boats. Impressed! You can't believe how impressed I was or you would have been if you had been there.

The Petrof Bay dropped anchor amongst the "big boys": the battleships and carriers and right along side the Indiana. It was late afternoon so I decided that I would wait until the next morning and try to catch a motor launch or a mail boat for a ride over to the Indiana and surprise Melv. Early the next morning I awoke, went out on deck and "lo and behold", it was gone. Not only the Indiana but the whole damned "fast fleet" was gone. All the new battleships, big carriers, new cruisers, new destroyers and their support vessels were gone.

All that was left in the harbor were the escort carriers, old battlewagons, old cruisers and an array of destroyers and invasion vessels. The big fleet had left for a strike at Japan and place a defensive force between the next island scheduled for invasion and Japan. This island was to be Okinawa. What was left in the harbor was the invasion force and it was loaded and ready to go in a matter of a few days. I, the squadron, and the Petrof Bay were a part of that force. So again I had missed Melv. Maybe it was a good thing, had I gone over the night before, I might have stayed all night and spent a considerable time on a battleship and not with the blessing of the Navy.

For the few days we were at Ulithi anchorage we were anchored 26 miles from the island called "Mog Mog". Other than the warm beer, one of the two things I remember about Mog Mog was how high the beer cans were piled. I guess when you pour beer down the throats of a couple hundred thousand sailors and marines, even for a few days, its not hard to make a mountain of beer cans. The other thing I remember was the native cemetery. The bodies were buried on top of the ground under slabs of rock. This was because the elevation was probably three feet high and the bodies won't stay under the surface of the ground due to water level. It reminded me of the cemetery that Bloski and I visited in New Orleans.

On the last evening we were in the Ulithi anchorage, several of us caught a LCT and rode to the island called Falalop to go to a movie and just get off the ship for a couple of hours. Falalop was another of the atolls like Mog Mog that lie in a circle and formed an anchorage that was capable of harboring very nearly the entire United States Navy. This island contained the only air strip around the anchorage and was operated by a Marine squadron. It was on the way in to Falalop that we were to see the USS Randolph, CV-15. The Randolph had been left behind by the fast fleet because of a big hole in her flight deck. On the day before we arrived at Ulithi a couple of Japanese planes flew in from Yap Island a couple of hundred miles away. One dove into the flight deck of the Randolph and the other dove into the runway on Falalop, probably thinking it was the flight deck of a carrier. I'll bet that guy was sure surprised for a few seconds!

We were to be at the boat landing to meet the LCT at 2200 hours. We left the movie at 2130 hours and was at the landing about five minutes later. No LCT! It had already left and wasn't even in sight. There were several of us and we lodged a loud complaint with the harbor master. The basis of our argument was that the invasion fleet was to hoist anchor before dawn the next morning and we were suppose to be going with it. The harbor master knew this was true and called for a PT boat and we were treated to about a twenty mile ride at fast clip. Don't think this was PT-109, though, unless they resurrected it.

19

MARCH 21, 1945 -- MAY 26, 1945
OKINAWA OPERATION

The following morning the entire 7th fleet sailed from Ulithi. Once at sea

we were to see no other ships other than our force of escort carriers and

their escort destroyers. My first view of the CVEs was a line of twelve

carriers from horizon to horizon. I don't know how many there actually

were in that line but I do know that our particular force was made up of

eighteen CVEs and that we would be operating in three groups of six.

We arrived on station about sixty to eighty miles southeast of Okinawa

where the ships would remain for the next ninety days. All of our flight

operations would originate from this area. The only times the ship would

leave this area would be to rearm from the supply ships at Kerama Retta,

a group of small islands about 10 miles west of Okinawa that formed an anchorage. These islands were invaded and secured for that purpose. We arrived on March 25th and began combat missions that day against Kerama Retta and Okinawa. It only took a couple of days to secure the anchorage and for the supply ships and troop ships to move in.

R. H. Allison above USS Petrof Bay

The first combat mission against Kerama Retta involved a flight of fighter planes from VC-93. It was on one of the strafing runs that an antiaircraft shell burst under the plane of Ensign Tony LaMarco. A piece of shrapnel pierced the plane and struck Tony in the butt causing him to be grounded for several days. This was the first causality due to enemy action to be suffered by the squadron. He survived, but unfortunately the wound leaves a scar where Tony will not be able to show it off---- I don't think?

On April 1, 1945 the invasion of Okinawa began and I was in the first flight from the Petrof Bay to give direct support to the Marines landing on the beach. The landing took place about a mile from Yontan, the Japanese air field. Because we were flying in from the sea and directly over the air field we were able to strafe building, planes and anything else that came in our sights. I'm sure that the planes we saw and strafed had been shot at before but there was a certain amount of enjoyment in making the runs. On one run I saw a fire break out under a camouflage netting. Even though I didn't have any idea what other damage I might have caused or how effective we were in supporting the Marines, I know that I had left something burning.

On our final run we started at 10,000 feet making a run on the field firing all the way down. When we leveled off at about 100 feet I held the trigger down all the way across the field and firing at a control tower as we pulled up over the hills on the north side of field. When I released the trigger the guns were so hot that they kept right on firing. The other three planes in my flight made a left turn that took them over the landing craft coming into the beach. I was forced to fly straight ahead until all my ammunition was expended so that I would not endanger the landing force. I never found out but I'll bet there were four 50 caliber machine guns that were of no use after that.

Although many of our flights were uneventful, especially the local combat air patrols (LCAP), there were enough eventful ones to give my adventuresome soul a lifetime of memories. The uneventful flights do not stick in my memory but a majority of the target combat air patrols (TCAP) flights usually had something that I will never forget, especially those that end up in disaster or near disaster. The first combat death that occurred was on March 27th when a burst of antiaircraft fire exploded just behind the ball turret of a TBM. The turret was occupied by the gunner Price Seferian. He was killed instantly and his blood ran down into the radio compartment on the radioman. He was buried that evening from the fantail of the ship with the ship's company in attendance. That was the first service at sea I was to observe but would not be the last. Most of the deaths occurred when a plane was lost at sea and no one returned.

Three days later Ensign Gordon Collipriest was killed in a mid-air collision with a plane from another squadron. For some reason he wasn't missed until his group landed and he wasn't there. A short time later the other pilot involved made it back to his ship and reported the collision.

Ensign G. Alan Collipriest

Twenty one years later my wife, son, daughter and I were vacationing in Hawaii where we visited the Punch Bowl cemetery. On a wall where all the servicemen that are missing in the pacific are listed, the names of our missing are listed with the exception of Ensign Collipriest. Don't understand why!

Ensign Charles Janson

On April 12, the day President Roosevelt died, Ensign Janson, whom I mentioned earlier in our double dating adventures in Long Beach, was also killed in a midair collision. Because of the interesting story that goes with this accident I will relate it later. On June 15th Ensign George Vigeant was killed when his plane exploded while making a water landing after being hit by antiaircraft fire. On July 20th Airman A.R. Katough was drowned when the TBM he was riding in crashed while taking off the carrier. He was pinned in the plane when it was struck by the carrier. The pilot and gunner got him out and aboard the rescue destroyer but they were unable to revive him.

My squadron lost several planes at the hands of the enemy and I am willing to bet that we lost more without their help. Certainly we lost more than double the number that we are credited with shooting down.

On the 31st of March, I was to make an aborted takeoff and a water landing but not of the variety of controlled landings a pilot likes to make whether good or bad. This takeoff was bad! As a matter of fact it wasn't a takeoff, it was a crash! Who or what was at fault? Who's to say! I would probably get an argument but as far as I am concerned the crash was due to circumstances beyond my control. The sequence of events leading up to the crash and the experience of the crash goes exactly like this: The skipper's division in which I was in the fourth plane was scheduled for a pre-invasion strafing mission on Okinawa. The weather was very heavy and when we were called to man the planes the ship was rolling from one side to the other with about a 12 degree roll. While I was sitting in the plane waiting for my turn to do a fly-away takeoff I could look out the right side of the plane and be looking very nearly straight down into the water. This was partly due to the hydraulic shock absorbers on the landing gear, which allowed the plane to roll even more than the 12 degrees of the ship. Then I would look out the left side and see nothing but blue sky. In the next minute the ship would roll to port and I would look out the left

136

side and see water and the right side and see sky. My position on deck at the time was slightly right of the fore and aft center line of the deck and at an angle of about 30 degrees to that line. When it came my turn to be positioned for takeoff the deck officer directed me to the center of the deck but left me spotted at that 30 degree angle. There I got the signals for checking the engine and the two finger wind up (full power) and the signal to release the brakes and go. I did. Unfortunately the tail of the plane was down hill on a starboard roll. With full throttle and hard right brake I could not get the plane lined with the deck. By the time the ship had rolled even keel the plane was very close to the port side. I had an instant to decide whether to go ahead and try to gain control or used the brakes and try to stop. My instant analysis of the situation was that if the right brake didn't work before then why should it work now? And if the left brake does work then I'm going to cartwheel this plane over the side. The other option was to continue on and try to gain control with the engine, the right brake (if any) and the rudder. I opted the second. The rudder never had a chance to take effect and the plane continued at its 30 degree angle right over the side.

I pause here to say that if that deck officer had spotted me straight down the deck or had given me the release sign when the roll of the ship was approaching an even keel then none of this would have happened and I would have completed the mission. No one was injured.

The plane went over the side the ship just aft of the port stack and just forward of a 20 millimeter gun mount. The left wing struck the gun and spun it like a top. The port droppable gas tank was torn off and 60 gallons of 100 octane gasoline was sprayed down the catwalk and under the flight deck. Fortunately, the fuel did not ignite and all the deck hands had scattered to safer places.

The plane continued over the safety rail, nosed down, dove through the radio antennas and smashed nose first into the sea. The first thought I remember having after the decision to go ahead with the takeoff was to get out of the plane. Waves were breaking over the top of the cockpit and water was gushing in on top of me. I reached down, unhooked the safety belt and began to crawl out of the cockpit. Because of the water I couldn't see anything and was totally outside the plane when I found that I couldn't go any further. Not knowing or seeing what was causing the problem, I climbed back into the plane and sat down. By this time the cockpit and I were under water and I came up straight out of the cockpit with no trouble. I could look up and see the surface of the water. I was not too deep and had no problem getting to the surface. This was the first of two occasions I was to use the experience of the "Delbert Dunker".

Once on the surface I looked around and saw the carrier moving away from me at some distance. At this time I decided to inflate my "Mae West" (life jacket). I reached down pulled the lanyards on the CO_2 bottles and the jacket inflated. Unfortunately, I had not unsnapped the parachute harness and I was immediately squeezed in the harness. After getting out of the harness I decided to get out the two-man raft which was attached to my parachute pack. The parachute and raft were used to sit on when in the plane.

At this point I think it is necessary to explain why I had my parachute and raft with me. They should have been with the plane slowly sinking to the bottom of the sea or floating somewhere other than on my bottom. I now knew why I had been hung up in the plane. I had not unhooked the two front strap snaps of the chute from the harness. The parachute with the package containing the raft and survival gear is a separate unit from the parachute harness. The parachute and raft unit is a part of the plane equipment and is in the plane when you climb in the cockpit. The parachute harness is a part of the pilot's gear. It is adjusted to his size and remains with him through out his tour of duty aboard the carrier. He is wearing the harness when he enters the plane and it is only necessary to connect four snaps to make a single unit of the chute, the raft, the harness and the pilot.

The standard procedure was not to hook up these four snaps until you are airborne so that you will be less encumbered in case of entering the water after an aborted takeoff for any of a million reasons. My routine had been to hook just the two front snaps, then hook up the safety belt, then unhook and lay the parachute straps across the safety belt so that they would be handy once I was airborne. If the safety belt was hooked first, the straps would be somewhere below the seat and I had found it to be irritating to be searching for these straps in the bottom of the plane while trying to take a position with the other planes in my flight. This procedure had worked out very well for me except for this one occasion when I had neglected to unhook the straps. The result of this over sight was that when I was crawling out of the plane the parachute and raft were trailing along behind and became lodged between the side of the plane and the wind shield. This prevented me from being able to remove myself from the cockpit. Upon reentering the plane and sitting down then coming straight up and out of the cockpit, the chute and raft followed along very nicely. It was a hard and embarrassing lesson but not so embarrassing that I would not share the dumb experience with the other members of the squadron in hopes that someone else would not get caught up in a similar situation.

Five photo sequence of failed takeoff

NO. 464-3 DATE MAR 31 1945

UNIT U. S. S. PETROF BAY (CVE 80)

MADE FOR Air Dept.

SUBJECT Water crash of # 17

OFFICIAL PHOTOGRAPH
NOT TO BE USED FOR PUBLICATION
BY ORDER OF
THE CHIEF OF THE BUREAU
OF AERONAUTICS

CONFIDENTIAL

Backside of previous photo

Once I was free of the harness I remembered seeing something in the water while I was watching the carrier sail away. Another look around revealed a ship's raft floating about 25 feet away from me. The plane had knocked it off the railing as we went over. This was a big raft that was designed for 50 men in case of abandoning ship. No two man raft for me! I swam to the big raft, climbed up on it and watched the Petrof Bay fade away. In a matter of a few minutes a destroyer, the USS Lardner that was part of the carrier screen, came slowly sliding through the water and threw me a line. I lashed the line to the raft and the raft swung into the side. The DD had a cargo net slung over the side and two big burly sailors were clinging to it. As I grabbed the net they grabbed me and the next thing I knew I was on the deck. I was not injured or tired but they absolutely insisted that I lie down in a first-aid basket and be carried to sick bay which turned out to be the Captain's cabin. To resist was absolutely futile, so I complied. I had to lie down on his bunk and in a couple of minutes I discovered the reason for all the attention, in came a pharmacist mate with the medicinal brandy, enough for everybody. There had to be at least a dozen guys in that cabin for a two ounce bottle of brandy.

They were a considerate bunch of swabs, cleaned and oiled my gun and washed and dried my flight suit. In about a half an hour the destroyer was up along the starboard side of the carrier and I was returned to the Petrof Bay in a breeches buoy suspended between the destroyer and the fantail of the carrier. I was told before leaving the Lardner they had bent their crane on the stern trying to hoist the raft aboard.

Three and a half hours later I'm up on the signal bridge of the island to watch the skipper and the rest of my flight return to land aboard when a signalman pointed to the water on the port side of the ship in exactly the same place I had gone over four hours earlier. There was the biggest damned shark I have ever seen anywhere cruising along side the ship. I don't know where he had come from but I'm willing to bet that he wasn't very far away while I was splashing around earlier. This shark or at least the thought of it will come up again before I'm through with this story.

Since the end of the war, it has been brought to my attention that the destroyer sailors who plucked "downed" aviators from the sea and returned them to their carriers in exchange for 10 to 20 gallons of ice cream, considered the value of the aviator as about the same as the price of the ice cream, about two-bits a quart or about ten to twenty dollars.

The aviator on the other hand may well have appreciated being plucked from the sea by the sailors who have just saved his butt from being shark bait. But he might have been the aviator who had shot down a kamikaze that might well have saved the same sailors from having their butts singed.

So the aviator considers himself as being worth his weight in gold, thirty five dollars on the gold standard that existed during the war or three hundred dollars an ounce on today's market. Perhaps he was worth more as twenty gallons or 160 pounds of yellow gold--ice cream that is! For that is one precious item the carriers had that the destroyers did not have-ice cream!!!

It so happened that the plane I drove over the side was number 17. This one happened to have been the plane with my name printed on the side under the cockpit. The plane numbers were assigned according to the seniority of the fighter pilots. It was also the photo reconn plane with all the cameras for a fighter plane mounted in the fuselage. This is the reason I was not to fly any photo missions. It was some kind of a coincidence that this plane was in the right place on the deck for me to be assigned to it. Almost without exception we were assigned to planes as our names appeared on the flight schedule. The planes were lined up in a random fashion.

After the crash I was taking in a little sun on the forecastle and was having a conversation with one of the ship's navigation officers. He informed me that the depth of the ocean in the area of the crash was 1500 fathoms-- that is 9000 feet deep. Part of the subject under discussion was: What is the density of the water at a 9000 foot depth and will the plane sink to the bottom or sink to a depth where the density of the steel and the density of the water are the same and will the plane just float until it runs aground or continue to sink to the bottom. We didn't come to a conclusion as to the density of the water at a great depth but did agree that the plane would sink to the bottom.

On April 3rd, I was assigned to a flight in a division lead by Lieutenant Varney Lieb. This, again, was a pre-dawn flight. It was back to the fly-away takeoff again. Again it was a solid black night. We were launched and rendezvoused. At 1,000 feet we were placed on a vector to intercept a bogey coming in from the west just above the water. The fighter director was on our own ship, the Petrof Bay. Our ship had been detached from the formation of six carriers and was 10 miles outside the Kerama Retta anchorage waiting for dawn to go in and rearm. The vector we received placed us on a course that took us directly over the anchorage. Because of the bogey the condition was "Flash Red". Needless to say, when we reached the anchorage every ship in the anchorage opened fire on us. With shock and extremely fast reactions, the four planes dispersed themselves in four different directions. My immediate thought was that the quickest way out was the way we came in. I reversed course and dove the plane to gain speed. The tracers from the 30 caliber machine guns, the fifty calibers, the 20 mm, the 40 mm, the 3 inch cannons and the five inch cannons chased me for a considerable distance. My plane wasn't touched nor were any of the other three. Lt. Lieb called for us to rendezvous again a few miles south of the island. By the time we got together it was daylight and we could see a black cloud over the anchorage where we had

been fired upon.

It was by this time the end of our flight period and we were given a vector

of 090 degrees to return and land on the USS Tulagi CVE-72 since the

Petrof Bay was in the anchorage. Having gotten the direction to the ship,

Varney put us on course, trimmed the plane for level flight, pulled out a

cigarette, lit up and settled back for a leisure ride home. I was a little

puzzled and after a minute or two I Looked back at my wing man. He had

a puzzled look and shrugged his shoulders. Varney's wing man looked

back with a questioning look. I increased the speed of my plane, took over

the lead from Varney and reversed our course 180 degrees. For some

reason Varney had without thinking placed us on a course directly

opposite to direction of the ship. We were headed for China. We would

never have made it.

We would be on the Tulagi until the next morning at which time we were

scheduled for another pre-dawn LCAP flight. After this flight we would

return to the Petrof Bay which should be returning to the formation

during the night. We had nothing to do all day but wander the ship and sit

in the ready room. That evening we were having dinner in the wardroom with the Tulagi's squadron when "General Quarters" sounded. Everybody in the wardroom bailed out. One of the guys said to us on his way out that when this ship sounded "General Quarters" the bogey would almost be in his dive. The four of us just sat there and finished dinner, then ambled up to the ready room. When we got inside we were informed that the Kamikaze had in fact dove on and struck the USS Wake Island, CVE-65. The previous night the Wake Island had taken the place of the Petrof Bay in the southwestern corner of the group of six destroyers. The following morning the Wake Island, with a hole in the forward end of her flight deck and one in the side of the hull where the plane had passed through, had departed for Pearl Harbor and the Petrof Bay was back on station in it's usual position. Strange turn of fate!

On April 6th my division was launched on a pre-dawn flight over the target. We were under the direction of a "fighter director". This is an officer on a "Picket" destroyer who with the aid of a radar screen will put you on a course to intercept incoming Kamikazes. We had several vectors that morning but could not make contact. If it sounds like we had lots of pre-dawn hops, it is true, more than our share because the skipper chose the times he wanted and these were the dawn and dusk flights when the

Kamikazes were the thickest. Our luck was just not good enough to make contact.

On this particular flight, immediately after takeoff, we were given a vector to intercept a bogey at sea level but could not find him. His altitude was changed to 3,000 feet with no luck, then to 15,000, no luck, then to 24,000 feet where a marine in an F4U shot the enemy down. Don't ask me whether this guy had been at 24,000 feet all the time or not. All I know is that if all our other information had been no better than this it's no wonder we couldn't find the enemy. Not everyone in our squadron was so unlucky, though. The squadron scored several victories.

All of our LCAP flights were relatively uninteresting contrary to the TCAP flights. On one TCAP occasion, we spent nearly four hours over the target area with no activity. Upon release by the fighter director the skipper requested permission to seek targets of opportunity in the enemy occupied portion of the island. He was given permission and we ran the island from north to south shooting at anything and everything we could see. This included houses, barns and any other structure that came in to view. It also included several objects that were circular in shape and appeared to be gun emplacements. In the center of each was a long slender barrel appearing object we took for a gun. Needless to say we poured quite a bit of ammunition on these things. Later we were to learn that these objects were grinding mills. The long shaft was a wooden pole that was tied to a horse walking in a circle rotating the grinding stone. Maybe a little embarrassing, but it was fun!

After reaching the end of the island we continued on a course to the southeast which would take us close to the carriers where we would pick up the homing signals on the radio and they would pick us up on radar. As we progressed the weather deteriorated and the ceiling reduced to less than four hundred feet. We were under the overcast and had been on the same course for more than enough time to have received these signals and even to have reached the ships. Nothing happened, no signals and the visibility was so bad we would literally have to hit the ships to see them. The skipper kept us on the same course for so long that I knew we had passed the ships. Dunagan knew this too, but we weren't second guessing the skipper, which at that time was a mistake. Anyhow, after a considerable time we came to a hole in the cloud cover and the skipper did a spiraling climb to gain altitude. When we reached an altitude of about 5000 feet we began to faintly receive the homing signal and the ships picked us up on radar. We were 80 miles southeast of the ships, just exactly twice as far as we should have gone.

We again descended through the over cast and about half way back Al Godfrey reported that the red light was on the reserve gas tank of his plane. This meant that he had about 20 gallon of fuel left. He had no sooner reported than the red light in my plane came on, followed by Dunagan's. It was to be a nip and tuck experience from there to the ship. If we were to run out of fuel we would have been in real trouble since the hour was late and daylight was fading. A water landing would be disastrous and the odds of being found were pretty slim or more likely non-existent.

We reached the ship and were given a straight in approach with Godfrey first since his light came on first. We all made a cut on the first approach. After securing the planes the gas tanks were checked. Godfrey had less than a gallon and I had slightly more than a gallon. It is very unlikely that neither Godfrey nor I could have taken a wave-off and still made a second pass to a landing. Had we not found that hole in the overcast the war would have ended for us that night. I don't know if the skipper said anything to the other two guys but he never mentioned our colossal error to me.

In the fore mentioned incident on April 12, one of the divisions of the other wing of our squadron was on TCAP several miles northwest of Okinawa. Enemy air activity was considerable that morning and this division was vectored to an incoming flight of Kamikazes. The division leader and his wingman took off after an enemy plane leaving the second section circling above. It wasn't long before they too spotted an enemy plane and engaged it. These two guys were Charlie Janson and Paul Bumgartner. Charlie slid in on the tail of the Japanese plane and Paul rather than getting involved held off to the side. While Charlie was firing away at the enemy an American F4U came screaming down from above and smashed into Charlie's plane. Both planes went into the ocean. Only one of the two pilots had bailed out. Bumgartner didn't know which man it was but followed the parachute to the water and continued circling while calling for a "Dumbo" (a PBY flying boat for rescuing downed pilots). Later we received word that it was the Marine who was rescued and Charlie was lost.

While Bumgartner was circling and being intent on keeping an eye on the downed pilot he suddenly began to find his plane disintegrating. His gun sight dropped into his lap, the instrument panel shattered, sheets of metal were being ripped from the wings of the plane. These things he could see and he knew he was being shot up. A glance in the review mirror revealed a Japanese plane sitting on his tail having a "Hey-day". Paul pulled a very erratic maneuver in an effort to shake the Japanese plane. It succeeded because the enemy did not follow him. Now Bumgartner found himself with a damaged plane with the oil pressure dropping. It was necessary for him to return to Okinawa and land at Yontan airfield which had been in American hands since the first day of the invasion. On his way back he came upon a "picket" destroyer. Observing the lack of oil pressure and increasing cylinder-head temperature, he decided to set the plane down in the water and ride back on the destroyer. He made his approach for the landing a short distance from the destroyer and when he was a few feet above the water the crew of the destroyer opened up on him and shot him the rest of the way into the water. The condition was "Flash Red" which gave them the right to shoot but it was hard to believe for me that the men on the destroyer were so poor at aircraft recognition that they couldn't identify a Navy plane, especially one at a short distance with the Navy insignia on it. Anyhow, he got out of the plane and in a few minutes a motor launch came up to him with a thirty caliber machine gun sticking in his face. They still didn't know that he was an American. At least they didn't shoot him in the water.

Bumgartner was returned to Yontan where he was to wait until our ship sent one of our TBMs for him. Later that day Wells, in his TBM with me in my fighter flying escort, flew into Yontan, picked up Bumgartner and flew back to the Petrof Bay. Janson was listed as missing in action. You might remember, Janson was the guy who, with Wilda, double dated with Margie and me.

On May 5th one of our TBM Grumman Avengers, piloted by Lieutenant Joe Oliver, was struck in the right wing by a burst from Japanese artillery shell. This burst damaged the right wing that made it unsafe to bring aboard the carrier for a landing. The option was to land at Yontan airfield that had been taken from the enemy and was now being used by the Americans. Joe landed safely and was to spend the night at the field with his crew before being picked up by one of the other TBMs from our carrier and returned to the Petrof Bay. The plane remained at Yontan.

Lt. Joe Oliver and his damaged TBM

Just by coincidence it happened to be the day that the Japanese attacked the airfield with six bombers, each loaded with twenty soldiers. Four of the bombers were shot down before they could land and a fifth crashed on the field. All hundred troops and pilots were killed. The sixth crash landed on the runway where the twenty troops spewed out throwing hand grenades and firing rifles. They succeeded in destroying several American planes before being exterminated by the base Marines. In spite of the fire works, there were no American personnel killed or wounded.

While all this was going on Lieutenant Oliver and his crew, not being equipped to do combat took off for the woods to watch the fire works.

The next day Joe and his crew returned to the carrier and were once again back on the flying schedule.

During one of our DSG missions we were given a number from our grid maps and requested to strafe and fire rockets into this area as there was reported to be camouflaged vehicles and other enemy equipment there. We made several runs on the area but were unable to see much of anything because of the camouflaging and the dense jungle. I could see fire and smoke from the area but could not see what was burning. The skipper told the three of us to circle while he went in for a closer look. He had barely passed over the area when little black clouds began to appear behind his plane. At the same he could see tracer bullets flying past his plane. We called for him to get the hell out of there but it was unnecessary, he was well on his way. Never did find out what damaged we caused, but we were thanked and given a "Well done!" by the coordinator on the ground.

One of Wells' photo reconn flights was to do a strip photograph of the shore line and cliffs of the small island of Miyako Jima for the purpose of determining the strength of the fortifications. I was flying as his fighter escort. He was ordered to deliver the exposed film to the operations officer of Kadena airfield on Okinawa. After we landed and delivered the film, Wells thought it would be a good idea to take a tour of the local area that had already been secured. Somehow he managed to get a jeep with a Marine lieutenant for a guide. There wasn't much to see on this tour but a few native Okinawans. They were the old and the young and were contained in a wire enclosure. They certainly didn't appear to be much of a threat to anyone's safety.

Okinawa cemetery crypts
Lt. R Friedrick, Ensign J. Wells, Marine Lt., Airmen Fielder

The thing that makes the trip interesting was the burial tombs. These tombs were constructed of rock in the side of a hill. We could see them from the air. They at first appeared to be some kind of fortification and I have no doubt had received considerable explosive attention. These tombs were quite old and contained the ashes of the local former residents. Wouldn't you know that Wells would have to have one of the urns from one of the tombs for a souvenir. He crawled through a small opening, selected the one he wanted, dumped the ashes and hauled the urn back to the ship. Unfortunately for Wells, Doc. Starr tossed the thing over the side of the ship for health and safety reasons.

Japanese postcard found on Yontan

For a period of eight days during May our carrier and another were assigned to protect a fleet of oil tankers while they cruised north to about 200 miles off the Japanese coast where they were to refuel the "Fast Fleet". On this cruise just at dusk, a Japanese mine came floating through the formation of tankers and just a short distance off our port side. We stood on the flight deck and watched it pass by as a destroyer escort shadowed it. Once astern the formation of ships the escort opened fire and exploded it while still in our view.

It was on this cruise with the tankers that we were invaded by a pod of whales too. There were several of them and they were more or less laying on the surface of the water and kind of laced through the formation of ships. Even though they were among a lot of ships, none were hit. The ships didn't change their course nor did the whales.

The object of this escort duty was for the TBM pilots to fly antisubmarine patrols. They were to fly 200 miles out on one course do a 50 mile cross leg and fly back to the ship. On one of these legs there was a very small island held by a small detachment of Japanese soldiers. The island was too small for an airstrip so there were no plans to capture it. Our pilots were told to stay clear as these guys were armed and would shoot. The pilot who got the segment nearest the island was Jim Wells. He had his own ideas. He took the squadron photographer with him and sure enough, he flew over the island. Nothing happened during the first pass so he tried for two. Yes indeed! They opened up on him and punched several holes in his plane.

This extra distance that Wells had traveled, to disobey instructions, ran his fuel so low that by the time he got back to the ships he was practically on fumes. Since our carrier was not taking planes aboard at the time and one of the other formations of carriers was receiving planes, Wells got into their traffic circle and landed on one of those carriers. The landing was a little short and the tail wheel struck the curved portion of the after-end of the flight deck. This sprung the back of the plane rendering it temporarily unflyable. The Captain of that ship called Wells to the bridge wanting to know what the hell he was doing on his ship. Wells told him that he was nearly out of fuel and would not have been able to wait for the Petrof Bay's formation to start landing planes. The captain called to have the gas tank on Well's plane checked and the report was that there was only a cupful left.

Wells was off the hook on that score but he still had to get back to our ship and he didn't have a plane since his was damaged with a broken back, full of holes and grounded. You can believe it or not but he talked that captain into trading his plane for one of theirs and on the next flight flew the new one back to the Petrof Bay. For all, his shenanigans Wells was given three days in hack (restricted to his room). He was not to be lonely, he had eight roommates.

At some point in our daily operations, I began getting an uneasy feeling in the traffic circle when approaching for a landing, especially in the final turn into the stern of the carrier. This didn't happen once, but was getting to be a regular occurrence. The feeling I would get was that the plane was gradually rolling to the left and was about to roll right into the ocean. Not just one plane but any plane I happened to be flying. There seemed to be nothing I could do to stop the roll in that I had the stick as far to the right as it would go. By the grace of God I managed to get aboard each time. Not only was I concerned, but the landing signal officer was after me because I was not responding to his signals quickly enough. He was not able to offer me any constructive advice and I knew that I had to solve the situation or I was going to wind up in the water.

One day as I was experiencing this feeling, I decided to turn the plane loose and see what would happen. This moment came almost immediately. On the turn to the down wind leg at about 50 feet of altitude I again had the stick full right and was at the limit of my control. I pulled my feet off the rudder pedals and took my hand off the stick. I was no longer flying the plane, it was on it own. To my surprise the left wing came up and the plane leveled out and was flying very nicely, straight and level. I may be thick headed but it didn't take me but an instant to recognize what I had been doing. Being intent on following the procedures for the approach and landing I was, without being aware it, applying pressure to left rudder pedal causing the plane to roll and applying right aileron to hold the left wing up. This was cross controlling the plane. If I had been flying a straight line in place of turning I would have been slipping the plane just as I had done in slips to a circle. I was never to make that mistake again. Landings were normal again.

The squadron suffered at least 110 incidents of damage to its planes due to enemy antiaircraft fire. I am aware of only one time that my plane was hit by enemy gun fire. I became aware of that only after I landed and the plane captain pointed out a machine gun air scoop that had been split open. Was very minor and didn't interfere with the flight characteristics of the plane.

On one of our strafing missions on the islands of Miyako and Ishigaki Shima we were to bomb and strafe the airfields to damage the runways so that enemy aircraft could not fly in from Formosa, land, refuel and take off for Kamikaze runs on Okinawa. These were two very small islands about half way between Formosa and Okinawa. We would start our runs from about 10,000 feet and pull out just above the tree tops. In the dive of one of my runs, my plane began shaking and thrashing around so violently that I could no longer hold the stick, even with both hands. I assumed that I had taken a hit from AA fire and the plane was out of control and that I had no choice but to jump. I took my hands off the stick, reached for the canopy release. In a matter of seconds I needed to be out of the plane before it hit the ground. When I released the controls, the plane came out of its dive and began to lose airspeed. As it lost speed it became less the violent and I realized that I might again be able to get control. This did happen and at a lower speed I had normal control again. I circled the island until my flight had completed its runs, then I rejoined them. To fly with them I had to increase my airspeed to match theirs but this caused the severe vibrations to return. The skipper assigned one of the TBMs to escort me back to the ship while they went ahead of us. The rest of my flight and landing were normal. As soon as the plane was on the deck we scrutinized the plane for the cause of the trouble. What we found was that one of the connecting rods that tied the control wire from the stick to the trim tab on the elevator had stripped its treads and the tab was free to flop on its hinges. At low speeds there was little or no effect but at high speed as in a near vertical dive a small movement up and down would cause a great amount of movement in the forward end of the plane. It was this great amount of movement caused by a little flutter that I was experiencing.

A couple of years after the war had ended I read in the Des Moines newspaper that the Army had discovered the graves of nine Navy and Marine fliers who had been shot down and taken prisoner on these two islands. They were flown to Formosa and executed. I have no reason to doubt the story. Not only did I have trouble over these two islands but we lost three or four planes there. One crashed in the ocean and the pilot was killed. The other pilots were rescued by seaplanes or by a submarine. In fact, the skipper was shot down over these islands twice. The first time we were circling over him while he was in the water waiting for the "Dumbo" to show up. I was sure that the wrong coordinates were given for this location so when the "Dumbo" didn't show I kept looking in the direction that I expected it to be. Sure enough I spotted a very tiny dot in the sky to the west. I was not able to raise the leader of our flight on the radio, so without notifying Dunagan, I took off flew to the dot, discovered the dot to be the rescue plane and led it back. I've often wondered if we might have lost the skipper if I hadn't noticed the error in the coordinates. The second time the skipper was shot down over these islands he was picked up by a submarine and spent three weeks aboard before being

returned to Okinawa and back to the carrier.

20

MAY 26, 1945 -- JUNE 10, 1945.
REHABILATION CENTER -- GUAM

On May 30th the Petrof Bay returned to Guam where our squadron was transferred to the USS Steamer Bay, CVE-87. Before the Steamer Bay was to return to Okinawa it had to go into dry dock for 10 days. During this time the whole squadron was transferred to a flight rehabilitation center on the southern end of Guam some 20 miles from Agana where we had spent three weeks before. This was 10 days of relaxation, no flying, just swimming and lying around on a beach.

One day a group of the officers decided we should have a party and that we should invite some nurses and Red Cross women from Agana to the party. We didn't really believe that the women would come but why not try. Jim Wells volunteered to make the trip to Agana to make the pitch and conned me into going along. We checked out a bus from the motor pool and with the driver and we took off. Upon arriving at the women's compound the driver pulled in and parked in front of the office door.

As Wells and I dismounted from the front door of the bus we were blasted by the terrifying roar of aircraft engines, not one but several. We looked up and saw a B-29 coming straight at us. This plane was coming in to land and there was no runway ahead of him. It passed less than a hundred feet high, directly over our heads and the nurse's quarters. It then struck a telephone pole about 100 feet beyond us, passed right along side a NATS terminal. This building was always occupied by two or three hundred service men waiting for air transportation. There were three C-54s lined up next to the NATS terminal. The B-29 broke the antenna that runs from the tip of the vertical stabilizer to the cockpit on the first C-54. It then struck and sheared off the vertical stabilizer even with the top of the fuselage on the second C-54 and then sliced the top half of the fuselage of the third C-54 like the top half of a hot dog bun. The pilot of the B-29 was trying to make the taxi strip at the end of the two parallel runways of the Agana air field. Unfortunately, the taxi strip was occupied by a C-46 waiting to take the runway. The pilot of the B-29 swerved his plane to miss the C-46 and plowed into a grove of pine trees along side the C-46.

The B-29 was torn into a mass of wreckage and went up in flames. Wells, the bus driver and I took off on the run to view the scene of carnage. The only one to survive the crash was the tail gunner. I only know that he was pulled from the wreckage but I do not know if he survived. I don't know if there were any other casualties on the ground. Anyhow, there were the three of us and about five hundred other service people surrounding the wreckage watching the fire and listening to the exploding ammunition. I gave no thought to the possibilities of there being bombs left on that plane after its attack on Japan. I still can't understand why we were not more concerned.

We had work to do so back to the nurse's quarters. Wells, with his glib tongue, sold eight of these women on coming to the party. We journeyed back to the rest camp and had a very nice afternoon and evening before taking the women back to their quarters. I don't think there were any "Tailhook" incidents at that time. This guy, Wells, never ceased to amaze me with his abilities and his guts. One Friday, while we were at Los Alamitos, he checked out a TBM, flew to North Island air station in San Diego, picked up a Wave Ensign that he had met a couple of months before, flew her back to Los Alamitos, took her out on the town for the weekend and then flew her back to San Diego on Monday. Guts!!! Incidentally she was married.

Following the party, at which several guys got plastered, somewhere around three o'clock in the morning we were shaken out of our sleep by this blood curdling yell: "For Christ Sakes, get the hell out of here!". Someone turned on a light and there, standing at the end of Varney Lieb's bunk with him sitting up in bed, was "Dad" Dunsweiller. In his drunken condition he had to go to the head and in the dark had wondered into the end of Varney's bunk. There he cut loose, urinating right in the middle of Varney. Having been cut off in the middle, Dad staggered to the rear screen door of the Quonset hut, stepped out and fell down a flight of five steps. We heard the crash then nothing more. After a few minutes someone asked: "Do you think he might have hurt himself?" With that the guy, who asked the question, got up and looked. Dad was no where to be seen. This began a search around the camp sight for him. The concern for his safety was that armed guards patrolled the area to protect us from infiltrating Japanese soldiers who survived the invasion and were hiding in the hills. Dad was found several hundred yards from our hut unhurt but still under the influence.

21

JUNE 10, 1945 -- JULY 24, 1945
EMBARKED ABOARD USS SSTEAMER BAY
BACK TO THE WAR

While we were at this rest camp, a typhoon hit Okinawa and reeked havoc

with the invasion fleet. The cruiser Pittsburgh lost its bow and returned to

Guam to go into dry dock and have a temporary bow constructed for the

trip back to the states. This meant the Steamer Bay had to vacate the dry

dock. We were loaded aboard and returned to the battle where death

and mayhem was still in progress.

On June 15th I was scheduled for a TCAP mission. I was again in the fourth

plane to do a fly away takeoff. As per the usual procedure I ran up the

engine for its pre-take off check. Everything was normal with no

indications of any problems. On the signal from the deck officer I applied the power and began my run down the deck. About two thirds of the way down the deck the engine began detonating and would not increase power. I was beyond the point of no return and was forced to continue with an air speed that was considerably "iffy". I went off the end of the deck and the plane hung in a three point attitude but refused to climb. As a matter of fact it was settling closer and closer to the water. I had to hold the plane on a straight course to prevent a stall for as long as possible. I could look out either side and see the water licking at the bottom of the plane. I could not see anything in front of the plane but knew that one of the other carriers was directly ahead about three miles away. Not knowing how far I had traveled and knowing I was going to get wet I decided to set the plane down while I had control rather than stall and turn it over.

I pulled back on the throttle and immediately hit the water. The plane flipped on its back and I was under water again. This time I did not have my parachute attached to the harness, came out freely from the cockpit, came to the surface and looked around. The first thing I saw was one gigantic carrier bearing down on me and not far away. I took off swimming on a course 90 degrees to that of the carrier. I was having trouble doing the crawl stroke because of the waves and the parachute harness so I took to the sidestroke. I was a little off to the side when the bow passed even with me. I saw the bow of the ship strike the plane square on. Then I looked up and saw that I was still under the flight deck but far enough to the side to see the sailors in the catwalk motioning for me to keep swimming. They knew, as well as I, that the screws of the ship would suck the water and me under the ship and through the screws if I remained too close. At that moment I must have been about 20 feet to the side. I took off doing the sidestroke again and when I passed the stern of the ship I could have reached out and touched it. The screws do pull the water in!

I was on the starboard side of the ship when it passed. I was treading water as the waves from the wake of the ship were breaking over my head then suddenly I felt something touch the back of my head. With a start, I turned around fully expecting to find that shark that I had seen two months earlier staring me in the face. But, "Saints be praised", it was a little flame on the tip of a smoke bomb that had not yet began to smoke. It had been thrown off the stern of the ship as I passed. I have no idea if it ever smoked. Regardless, I was relieved.

Swimming is not exactly easy with clod hopper shoes on your feet so I began removing them. That wasn't easy either since I was exhausted from my swim. The first shoe untied easily and I struggled out of it. The other shoe string knotted and I was unable to get the shoe off so I forgot about it. Then, looking around again I spotted a four man rubber raft inflated and floating a short distance away. I took off after it and that wasn't easy since I was dog tired. I discovered that they had thrown the raft off the port side of the ship and down wind of me and moving away from me. This made the swim even longer and more tiring.

Having caught the raft I discovered that it is up side down and would have to be righted if I was to get in. This just wasn't about to happen. I didn't have enough energy left in me to turn that thing over. So I just stuck my arm through the rope attached to it and hung on waiting for the rescue destroyer, the USS Fleming, DE 32. It was not long in coming. As it passed by it was still making a little headway. The cargo net was hanging down the side but there weren't two big sailors hanging on it to give me a helping hand as there had been on the Lardner. As soon as I was close enough I grabbed the net and turned loose of the raft. I have no idea what happened to the raft but I'm sure they picked it up. When I grabbed the net, because of the forward motion of the ship I was dragged under the water. I hung on and began climbing. The deck is only five or six feet above the water, but in my worn out condition it was a mile. Not only did they not help me up the net they made me walk to sick bay. I would have gladly lain down in the basket this time. Not only did I suffer these indignities but also I had to wear a wet flight suit until I was back on the Steamer Bay. Don't get me wrong, I'm glad they were there.

On this same day, Lt. (j.g.) George Vigeant's plane was struck by enemy antiaircraft fire and he was forced to make a water landing. As he was about to sit down on the water his plane exploded. He was lost at sea and was the final fatality for the squadron. In all the squadron lost five fighter pilots and two TBM air crewmen in the year and a half that it had been in commission.

Ensign George Vigeant

The morning after my crash on the 15th, I was scheduled for a pre-dawn patrol with the skipper, Dunagan and Godfrey. Having lost my plotting board and all the maps and codes, I went the night before to the ACI (Aircraft Combat Intelligence) office to replace the missing literature. Lieutenant Bob Winters, the officer in charge, fixed me up with the board and most of the papers but said they were out of some and would get them to me.

About 0300 the morning of June 16th we were called to man our planes. Again this morning as it had been the day before the sky was black, the weather was lousy, it was raining and the ceiling was about 500 feet. This morning we were to be catapulted off the deck. After checking out the planes we were guided on to the catapult one at a time. The skipper, Godfrey and Dunagan were launched and I was spotted on the catapult and hooked up. After getting the 1 finger windup and checking the magnetos, I received the signal for the two-finger windup. There I sat with full power, feet off the brakes, right hand on the stick, right elbow in my gut and my head back against the headrest. I was ready to go. Nothing was happening. I glanced out the right side of the cockpit and saw the deck officer giving me the cut engine sign. Then I heard the radio telling me to cut the engine and sit tight that there was a bogey in the vicinity and the condition was "flash red". I sat there in the rain for about five minutes before I got the OK to start my engine. The other three guys had rendezvoused and were waiting for me some where beyond the formation of ships. This time when I was ready I was launched. I began to climb the plane to an altitude of three thousand feet where the skipper was supposed to be. I could not locate them so he said to meet them at target at point sugar. I replied with the affirmative. Again we were in the "flash red" condition and wouldn't you know that I would spot this orange glow. As far as I knew I was the only plane in the area so who or what was this orange glow? I was fairly close to it but the night was absolutely black and I could not see a plane. I know that it wasn't an American because the exhaust flames of our planes are blue. It could be the Japanese bogey because their exhaust flames are red or orange due to the inferior quality of the fuel. It could be a fire on a ship on the water which for me to identify would require me to fly back into the "flash red" zone. Common sense prevailed over heroism and I said to hell with it and took off for Okinawa. A later inquiry revealed that there were no fires on the ocean so maybe I missed my chance to score a "Kill". Too bad! I'm not sorry.

So now I'm on my way to point sugar. But where is point sugar? I pull out the plotting board, open it and "lo and behold!" no map indicating our rendezvous points. It was one of the papers they were out of and I wasn't smart enough to have checked. Well, I racked my mind to recall from previous flights where this point might be. I seemed to recall that it was about half way up the length of the island and on the west side. OK! I'll try it. I arrived at the place where I thought I should be but there is no skipper. This time he called over the radio to tell me they were about 5 miles due south of the southern tip of the island and circling. I would have to fly back across the island down the east coast for about 35 miles to get to them.

On the way down the east side I hear over the radio a message to a division of planes from another squadron from a command ship that there was a bogey on their radar screen about five miles from their ship at 3000 feet. Beings this was the area where I happened to be at that moment I became very alert. I looked down and could see the command ship and almost knew that they had me spotted as their bogey. I checked my IFF (identification, friend or foe) and it was on. I should have been recognized as a friendly. For safety's sake I kept watch for the division of our fighters and made a three hundred and sixty degree circle a few times looking for a bogey. The enemy had been known to slip up under an American plane, gain the protection of the IFF and move right into a formation of ships and make their Kamikaze run. I did not find any bogey and finally arrived under the over cast at the south end of the island. I eventually found the skipper still circling in a hole in the clouds. Upon joining up with them we returned to the carrier having fired not a single shot. I don't think he was too happy and I'll be damned if I was going to tell him about the map.

Our sorties against the enemy continued until July 24th at which time we and the Steamer Bay were ordered back to San Diego. The squadron was scheduled for decommissioning.

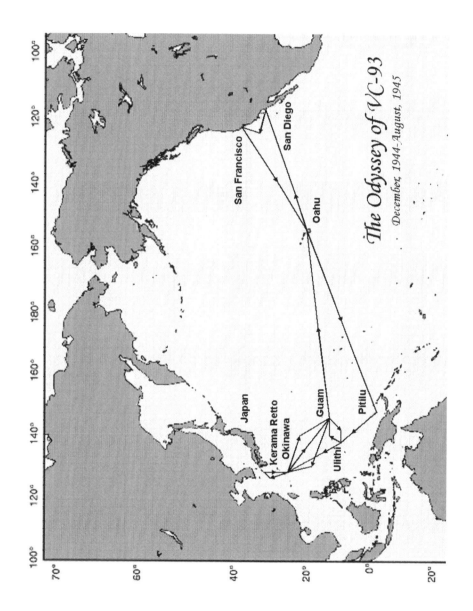

The Odyssey of VC-93
December, 1944-August, 1945

San Francisco
San Diego
Oahu
Japan
Kerama Retto
Okinawa
Guam
Ulithi
Pitilu

22

JULY 24, 1945 -- DECEMBER 15, 1945
FINAL DAYS OF THE WAR!

In the time span from March 25th to July 24th the squadron, both fighters

and bombers, had flown 2360 missions and had 110 incidents of damage

to its planes by enemy antiaircraft fire. The squadron is credited with

having shot down 17 enemy aircraft while losing only one to a Japanese

plane. My particular contribution to the war effort was 54 missions. How

much damage I caused I cannot say because it is impossible to assess

damage to something that is behind you. I have always been skeptical of

the glowing reports of anyone flying a plane. I fired thousands of rounds

of ammunition, fired dozens of rockets, dropped several napalm bombs

and several 100 pound bombs on designated enemy targets with a

reasonable amount of accuracy. But in the jungle and camouflage areas I could not look back and leisurely estimate the damage. Planes in the sky or on a runway, or boats on the sea, or large barracks, or man made structures you can see and maybe assess damage. On Okinawa, by the time the invasion started the towns were demolished and the Japanese soldiers did not live in barracks at this time. Still, I feel we did what we had been sent there for and I am satisfied that the squadron deserved the "Well done" as received from fleet commander.

During our cruise from Pearl Harbor to San Diego we received word that the atomic bombs had been dropped on Japan. I'm sure we must have thought that the war was nearly over and must have wondered what was in store for us. I just don't remember. Upon arrival in San Diego the squadron was decommissioned. I received a thirty day leave and headed for Port Orchard, Washington where my family was now living.

On the way to Washington I spent a few days in San Francisco, enjoying what I consider the most fun town in the US with the girl I had acquired a very warm feeling for. This was Margie, whom I dated in Los Angeles. While I was over seas, she and three of her girl friend nurses had joined the Army Nurse Corps and were stationed at Letterman General Hospital in San Francisco.

Lt. Margie F. Wada, ANC

I arrived in San Francisco on the 16th of August, the day after Japan surrendered. The night before, August 15th, had been one tremendous victory celebration in the USA and especially there in San Francisco. The servicemen, and probably the civilians too, had torn the downtown apart. Every window on Market Street had been broken and stores looted. The commander of the 12th Naval District and the Army commander had placed a restriction on all locally stationed personnel.

Since I was traveling on orders, we had no trouble being on the street. There were damned few service personnel and very few civilians but there were plenty of police and shore patrol.

As Margie and I were walking down the street two sailors were strolling along when one of them kicked a garbage can. It had hardly hit the ground when two shore patrol and a cop had them by the collar.

I returned to San Diego after the leave and was reassigned to Air Group 5 at Klamath Falls, Oregon. I was with the squadron for only two or three weeks when an announcement came out that those wishing to resign from the Navy could do so. The things that influenced my decision to resign were first: I was not an academy graduate. Not being an academy man limits advancement possibilities. Second, I was not a college graduate and that too would limit my possibilities for an extended career. Third, I wasn't too sure I wanted to stay in the Navy for twenty years. So I requested to get out and was assigned to a CASU unit at NAS Pascal, Pascal, WA to await discharge.

With time heavy on my hands at Pascal I checked out an F6F, filed a flight plan to Kitsap County Airport in Port Orchard, Washington and flew there to visit my family. Guess the reason for this was to show off the big fighter plane that I had been flying, a little personal ego coming through again. This wasn't the first time they had witnessed their little boy flying. They had driven down to NAS Ottumwa to visit me while I was there in primary. It was fortunate I happened to be scheduled to fly that Sunday morning. The humorous part of the day was when we attended a program given for the local civilian people by the Navy, a teenage girl came up to me and asked for my autograph. I thought she must be nuts but my sisters, Marilyn and Helen thought it was great.

While at Pascal, I, and a dozen other pilots waiting with me, were assigned to ferrying planes to Clinton, Oklahoma, where the planes would be stored before being demolished. They were no longer needed for a war that didn't exist. The plane I was to fly had only about 10 hours on it and I wouldn't add much more time to it. The first leg of our flight was to Yakima, Washington a distance of 50 miles. We hardly got off the ground before we were landing. Spent the night in Yakima and left the next morning for Red Bluff, California. This flight was a little longer, maybe 300 miles. Arriving at Red Bluff the lead pilot (this was some guy who had been ferrying planes from the factory to the west coast and bumping guys like me off commercial flights with their number one priority, when they were ready to return to the factory.), ground looped his plane and tore up the wing tip. With an ulterior motive in mind, I volunteered to let him have my plane. He accepted and later that afternoon I crawled in the second seat of an SNJ and took off for NAS Alameda across the bay from San Francisco. For the next seven days and for every hour that Margie could get away from the hospital we would enjoy everything that San Francisco had to offer. The good thing was that I was on per diem drawing an additional seven dollars a day in addition to my base pay. After seven days I got a little self conscious and caught a NATS plane back to Pascal.

I was again assigned to another plane and followed the same route only this time after Red Bluff we flew to Madera, CA, Holtville, CA, Tucson, AZ, El Paso, TX, Midland, TX and finally Clinton. We spent the night at each of these fields. Seven days to get there. If we had taken a direct route we could have done it in one day. But we had time to kill.

It was on one of the return trips from Clinton, OK while I was with Margie in San Francisco, that we were walking down one of the streets in the center of town and I spotted this Naval Officer walking down the other side of the street, his hat cocked on the back of his head, his blouse hanging wide open in an unmilitary way and a woman hanging on his arm. For some reason his back looked familiar and I wanted to know if I truly recognized this guy. We crossed the street just as he and the woman turned into a bar. We followed them in and sure enough there sitting at the bar was Tom Hartshorn. He and I had gone all the way through high school together and were on the swimming team together. We swam naked during practice so maybe that is why I recognized his figure from the backside, plus the fact that we lived next door to each other for a few years. The three of us, minus the other woman (he had a wife back in Des Moines), spent the rest of the day together. I saw him once shortly after the war and called him on the phone a few years ago. He never returned my call and that was that! He died just a few months ago.

Another chance meeting happened on these SF junkets. While with Margie, I ran into Tom Bloski in the lobby of the Saint Francis Hotel. He had just returned from the pacific and was on his way home. From him I found out that Mike Michaelich and Sy Gonzalaz had survived the war but Bill Tuohimaa had been killed when his plane was shot down over Japan.

That afternoon, with Bloski and Margie and Margie's friend, Carmen from her nursing school days, went to the fleet landing where the USS Ticonderoga had tied up. Somewhere Bloski had gotten the word that our instructor from Green Cove Springs, Lieutenant Crommelin, was aboard. His squadron was attached to this ship. Unfortunately, he was a shore. We left a note just to let him know what had happened to his first students.

I had a Christmas card correspondence going with Bloski until about 1954 when his cards stopped coming. Some twenty years later on one of our driving vacations through the south, I looked up his phone number in the Pensacola directory and I called the number. The lady that answered gave me his number at the newspaper where he worked. I called, but the guy who answered didn't know me. It was Tom's son by the same name. He told me Tom senior had been killed in a helicopter crash in New Orleans in 1954.

I caught another NATS plane at Alameda for a flight to NAS Sand Point and Pascal, WA after spending the week courting Lieutenant Wada around our favorite liberty town. Another seven days on per diem. That was my last ferry flight. A few days later I was on a train headed for the Great Lakes

Naval Training Station and discharge. I was out of the Navy and on my way home on December 15, 1945, three years, five months and seven days after being sworn in to the Navy.

Did I ever see Lieutenant Wada again? Oh yeah! We were married fifteen months later on July 1, 1947, after she received her discharge from the Army Nurse Corps. She has been my heart and soul for the past fifty-one years.

Did I ever fly again? No! I have never flown a plane from that last flight to Clinton, Oklahoma. Did I enjoy flying? Absolutely. Why didn't I join the reserve and fly or do it privately? I was going to school and didn't have the time or the money. Do I regret the time I spent in the service? Absolutely not! It was one truly great experience. I would have hated to have missed it, but I wouldn't care to do it again and I certainly would not want my son or grandsons to have to go through any war.

Was I at any time frightened while flying? Just a couple of times. Once while at Los Alamitos I was flying wing on Bugs Dunagan in a rather lose, relaxed manner and a little wide of his wing tip. All of a sudden a couple of planes made an overhead pass on us. One of the planes, I'll swear, went between Dunagan's plane and mine. I'm sure the "Nut" driving that thing was not aware of my plane. What was not needed anywhere, especially flying, was a bunch of "Smart Asses".

One type of flying that was scary was blind flying. One kind of flying blind was making a slow pull-out from a dive at high speed such as a gunnery run. This blindness is the result of blood draining from your head and eyes causing the temporary loss of vision. After the dive is completed the blood returns, your sight returns and all you have to do is locate the horizon to get your bearings. To avoid trouble while you are in this sightless condition is to hold the stick in the center with a little back pressure so that the plane will be coming up out of the dive when your vision returns. It is a funny sensation but not particularly dangerous.

Another spooky situation was flying in formation while climbing or descending through a heavily overcast sky or through a very dense cloud. You are intent on watching and holding your position on the plane you are flying wing on when all of a sudden you cannot see it or any of the other planes in the formation. Immediately you are on instruments and hoping to God that you don't fly into each other. The more dense the clouds and the longer you are blind the greater the chance of a collision. It is a great feeling to come out the other side and see the other planes at some distance from you- any distance, just so they are away. This I experienced many times and every time I was spooked.

Probably one of the most God-awful sensations to happen to you is to return to the carrier after dark and find the ship blacked out. If you are fortunate, there will be a little moonlight or maybe enough twilight to have a dim horizon or maybe a vague shadow of the ship. If none of these exist you will arrive on radio and radar. Your approach and landing procedure is accomplished by communicating with the ship by the radio and radar. Once in the landing pattern and on the down wind leg you are advised to make your turn into the cross wind leg and when you are about thirty degrees off the upwind leg you gain visual contact with the carrier. Up to this time you have been flying blind. When you sight the carrier all you see is a stick man. This is the LSO. His uniform is a flight suit with narrow strip of florescent cloth down each leg, one strip up the center of his torso and one out each of his arms. At the end of the arm strips is a round florescent circle with horizontal narrow strips of this florescent cloth. All you see are these florescent strips until you are very near being directly aft of the ship. At this time, if you are lucky, you will make out the outline of the deck of the ship by seeing lights spaced down each side of the flight deck. These lights are small and can only be seen from directly behind and slightly above the flight deck for security reasons. Don't think for a second that you are going to land between those lights on your own. Your vision and depth perception just aren't good enough. You place your faith in God and the man with the paddles. With your faith and his talent you will land safely aboard. When you feel the plane hit the deck and the cable brings the plane to stop you breath a deep, deep sigh of relief and mop the sweat from your brow. I had a few twilight landing but only one near dark landing. On this one I could barely make out the outline of the ship. It was close enough to being black. Thank God there were no more!

Twilight landing aboard USS Steamer Bay, CVE 87

It was not the standard practice to fly at night but did happen occasionally. If you were caught in this situation, you just pray that when you arrive at the carrier there is no rain or fog and the sea is relatively calm.

Many times I was apprehensive but I don't recall being frightened by any of my experiences. I can hardly believe that these pilots who flew early in the war were not scared out of their wits when the best plane the Navy had was the F4F Wildcat. The Wildcat was no match for the Japanese Mitsubishi Zero either in speed, in maneuverability or in numbers. The only advantage the Wildcat had going for it was its protective armament and the ability to take a lot of punishment. As a result the Navy losses were running fairly high. And as the old saying goes: "necessity is the mother of invention". The inventor who came along at this time was Commander John Thatch. Commander Thatch developed a defensive maneuver that made it possible for fighter pilots to meet the Japanese in combat and survive with considerably fewer losses. This maneuver was named after Commander Thatch and was called the "Thatch Weave".

The gist of this maneuver was to be applied when the Navy planes were attacked by a superior force of Japanese planes. If a section of two planes or a division of three or four planes was attacked, the planes would split into two sections and fly parallel courses to each other about a half mile apart. The pilots of the planes on the left would keep a visual observation of the area above, beyond, and below from twelve o'clock ahead to six o'clock behind on the right side of their course. The section on the right would keep a visual observation of the opposite half of the area. In this manner the entire sky is under complete observation.

Regardless of what direction the Japanese originated their attack one of the Navy sections would see the Japanese planes and would initiate a turn into the Japanese planes. The other Navy section would see the first Navy section and know they were being attacked. At this time they would turn in to meet the first section passing either over or under as indicated by the first section. The first section would bring their guns to bear on the Japanese planes in a head on run forcing the Japanese to break off their attack on section two. After passing the Japanese, the first section would either return to its original course or complete a one hundred and eighty degree turn. Section two would be alert to section one's actions and would follow suit, thus returning to their original positions abreast of each other ready to meet the next Japanese attack if necessary.

The "Thatch Weave" was very successful and undoubtedly saved many American lives. Not only was Commander Thatch highly respected for his contribution to the war effort, he was, also, an ace Navy pilot having shot down more than a few Japanese planes.

In trying to imagine how these early pilots might have felt flying into almost certain suicide, and how I might have reacted to the same situation, I consider the fact that although the enemy air opposition was greatly reduced, we were still flying into heavy antiaircraft fire. Never once did I consider ducking out because of fright. So I suspect that had I been one of these early pilots I, too, would have flown into a nest of Japanese planes with complete confidence that I would survive just as I'm sure they did. Death is something that happens to someone else.

One of the other pilots of the squadron had a quote that expresses my feeling for my experiences as well as he felt for his. It goes like this "When I tell people that I was a carrier pilot, regardless of whether they are pilots of one of the other less fortunate services, or a civilian pilot or an ordinary citizen, they always say that they are amazed that anyone could or would land on one of those "boats". Quite frankly so was I. As a matter of fact, every time I caught a wire I would say to myself: Hot Damn, you did it again!"

Many years later at the 45th reunion of my high school graduation I returned to Abraham Lincoln High to find that the school had honored all of its students who had served in the military during WW II by inscribing their names on the wall above the office doors. I could find everyone's name that I knew, including my brother Melv's, even though he had gone to East High his last year. The only name I did not find was mine. I guess after forty five years no one there could give a s--- about any of those who served much less whether someone's name was missing. Still, my feelings were hurt.

I suppose that over the years I might have been "pissed-off" many times and for many reasons. Other than the over sight by my high school, I think the thing that "pissed" me most was the fact that I flew 54 official missions in enemy occupied territory in direct support of our troops against the enemy and on target combat air patrol in areas occupied by enemy aircraft. Even though we were not fortunate enough to make contact with the enemy these TCAP's were qualifying flights for the Air Medal and the DFC.

By coincidence, George Bush, the future president, and I flew nearly the same number of missions. He flew 56 missions and lost only one plane of record and two aircrew men. I lost two planes but no aircrew men. He got his DFC and several air medals and a lot of back-patting for his war time service while he was president. Seems the Navy could at least match his medals.

I had, in fact, been recommended for the DFC and four Air Medals. The recommendation had been approved by A.E. Montgomery, Admiral, U. S. Navy. I received the Air Medal and one star in lieu of the second before being discharged. The other two Air Medals and the DFC never came.

At our first squadron reunion in 1984, the skipper confirmed that the medals I had not received and those in the squadron who also had not gotten theirs had been officially approved and we were eligible to receive them. Maybe one day I'll make an inquiry.

The squadron reunion held in 1984 was very successful. Every two years since we have repeated the reunion even though our ranks are being thinned severely.

As for my brother Melv, after the Pearl Harbor attack he returned to Norfolk, VA, where he was assigned to the newly commissioned USS

Indiana, BB 58. He was to remain on the Indiana to the end of the war. I

never could get him to talk about his experiences for his years in the Navy.

Chief Melvin W. Allison

Carl, on the other hand, would tell of his experiences at the drop of a pin.

After pre-pre-flight he was assigned to pre-flight in California and then to

primary at Livermore, CA. At this station he and the Navy parted company due to a disagreement between him and his instructor- that is a story in itself.

After leaving the Navy he went to work as a longshoreman in San Francisco. This lasted until he was accepted into the Army Air Corps cadet program.

Lt. Carl A. Allison

He was not trained in fighters, but became a multi-engine aircraft pilot. He was to remain in the Air Force for twenty years, flying every two and four engine plane they had up to the B-47.

After his retirement he continued to fly for Air America, which at the time was rumored to be a spy organization -- he never admitted or denied this rumor but was exposed to some very dangerous flying. This was in Laos and Viet Nam during the war. He followed this job with a position as Captain on a Douglas DC-8 for Japan Airlines, then to Shaw Airlines in Alaska, then to Scenic Airlines where he flew the 1927 Ford Tri-motor hauling passengers from Las Vegas for a scenic flight over and down through the Grand Canyon. From there he had a job flying government employees to an "area" in the Nevada desert in a Boeing 737. He is now retired from flying.

As a late addition to this story, on Valentine's Day, February 14, 1996, I received in the mail a package from the personnel department of the Navy that contained the DFC (Distinguished Flying Cross). Also included were another Air Medal, a World War II Medal, an Asiatic Pacific Theater Medal, an American Campaign Medal and a Presidential Unit Citation Ribbon. I didn't even inquire about anything but the DFC.

Robert H. Allison

Medals and Citations

Presidential Unit Citation	Navy Wings	Presidential Unit Citation
Air Medal	Distinguished Flying Cross	Air Medal
Asiatic=Pacific Campaign	WWII Medal	American Campaign

The following poem is the poem that was repeated by my roommate at

Pensacola. I can't say that I didn't like it because I can truthfully say that I,

too, had a euphoric feeling when I was hurtling my eager craft around and

through the sun bleached, whipped cream clouds. I don't recall putting out my hand and touching the face of God, but it is a strange elating

feeling.

HIGH FLIGHT

John MacGill, Royal Air Force

Oh; I've slipped the surly bounds of earth,

and danced the skies on laughter's silvered wings.

Sunward I've climbed and joined the tumbling mirth

of sun split clouds and done a hundred things

you have not dreamed of - wheeled and soared and swung

high in the sunlit silence, hovering there.

I've chased the shouting wind along and flung

my eager craft thru footless halls of air.

Up, up the long delirious, burning blue,

I've topped the wind swept heights with easy grace,

where never lark or even eagle flew.

and while with silent lifting mind I've trod

the high untrespassed sanctity of space,

put out my hand and touched the face of God.

The author in a VC-93, FM-2 Wildcat

VC-93, North Bend, OR, 8/1944

Pictured members of VC-93:

Front row	2nd row	3rd row
Thomas	Dennett	Schenk
Foster	Winter	Beam
Davenport	Dunsweiler	Sullivan
Schearer	Lieb	Reid
Metier	Myer	Brown
Hylsworth	Gibbs	Hawley
Hughes	Smith	Oliver
Williams	Star	Vigeant
Godfrey	Skinner	Tuttle
Costa	Friedrick	Siewert
	Holcomb	Gainthrop
	Spurlock	Koop
	Parsons	Simidth
	Dunnagan	DeVries
		Sherlock
		Tushner
		Kinnaird
		Allison

EPILOGUE

THE RESTORATION OF A VC-93 AIRCRAFT
FM-2 WILDCAT, BUREAU NUMBER 74512

We were very surprised and pleased to learn in August of 1999 that an aircraft assigned to Squadron VC-93 back in 1945 still exists and is undergoing restoration at the Museum of Flight in Seattle, WA. What a marvelous coincidence that one of very few surviving FM-2s was flown into combat in 1945 by the author. In fact, it could very well be the only remaining FM-2 that actually saw combat since most surviving WWII era aircraft didn't arrive in the war zone before the hostilities ended.

Mr. Milt James, who was in charge of the restoration at the time, was interested in contacting a pilot who served aboard the aircraft carrier, USS Petrof Bay, CVE 80, and who had flown an FM-2, preferably the aircraft in his possession. In his search on the Internet, he found a website titled

Robert H. Allison

"CVE-80 U.S.S. Petrof Bay" by Mr. Ivor Jeffreys. In this website Mr. James discovered that Mr. Jeffreys' father had served on the Petrof Bay and was a member of the squadron VC-93 at the time the aircraft in question was operating from the carrier. Being that Mr. Jeffreys' father was a TBM pilot and did not fly the FM-2, Mr. Jeffreys directed Mr. James to me. Mr. James sent an E-mail to me requesting any assistance I could give him concerning the combat history of his FM-2. A correspondence has followed and it has been my pleasure to add my experiences with VC-93 and his aircraft to his endeavor.

The pictures seen below are of an airplane that served in the war in the Pacific during the Okinawa operation in 1945. The aircraft was delivered to the navy on December 29, 1944 at Trenton, NJ (the aircraft was manufactured at the Eastern Aircraft Plant in Linden, NJ). It left San Diego in January of 1945 aboard a transport carrier and off loaded at Apra Harbor on the island of Guam in the Mariana Islands in February. A short time later, on March 10th, 1945, it was loaded aboard the escort carrier, USS Petrof Bay, CVE 80. At the same time Composite Squadron VC-93 was assigned to the Petrof Bay. The Petrof Bay departed Apra Harbor for Ulithi anchorage where it joined the rest of the American Pacific fleet that was being assembled for the invasion of Okinawa.

208

On 25th of March this aircraft began its attacks on the Japanese islands and in aerial combat with the Japanese air forces, especially the Kamikazes. The assignments for this aircraft were Local Combat Air Patrol (LCAP), Target Combat Air Patrol (TCAP), and Direct Support Group (DSG is a flight of planes, either fighters, bombers or both directed to strafe and bomb the enemy in advance and support of the Marine and Army ground troops).

The author's flight log shows that this aircraft was flown by the author on two occasions. The first time was on April 22, 1945. This mission was local air patrol and lasted 3.9 hours. On May 20, the author flew another LCAP mission lasting 3.3 hours in this aircraft. Both flights were in the Okinawa area during the time the invasion was raging.

Squadron VC-93 was credited with the destruction of 17 enemy aircraft while in flight. Although it is known which pilots got the credit, there is no record of which plane he was flying. So it is possible that guns of this plane were the ones that shot down three of the enemy on one flight and possibly more on the other flights. This plane was one of twenty fighter aircraft on board the Petrof Bay that participated in approximately 1400 sorties averaging about 70 flights per plane. There were thirty fighter pilots in the squadron, in all probability, each of these pilots flew this particular aircraft at least once and most of the pilots more than once due to the random positioning of the aircraft on the flight deck and the assignment of plane numbers to each pilot as his name appeared on the flight information board in the ready room.

In the last week of May, the Petrof Bay was relieved of combat duty and sailed for the States stopping in Apra Harbor on the first day of June. This aircraft was off loaded and assigned to the maintenance facility on Guam at that time.

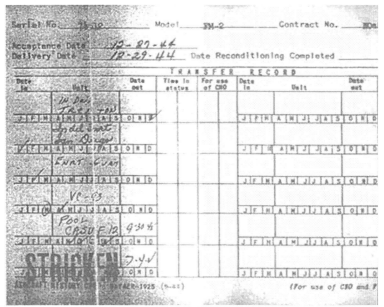

Aircraft History Card for FM-2, BU 74512

The history of this plane is unknown from September 1945 until 1949 when it was given to the Tacoma Naval and Marine Corps Reserve Training Center. For the next ten years it became derelict and then was presented to the King County Parks and Recreation Board. It was placed on the White Center playground in the Seattle area where it was kicked around for another ten years. At this time the plane came under the control of the Museum of Flight.

Aircraft at White Center Playground, 1959-1970

In the next 25 years, several attempts by various organizations were made to restore the plane to its original condition. These efforts failed. The plane returned to The Museum of Flight where it is now undergoing restoration. This plane is on view while being restored at the restoration hanger located about one mile south of the Everett Boeing Plant in Everett, WA.

The aircraft being stripped down

There are believed to be approximately 45 Wildcats on display in the world. Over 7800 were built in several varieties, the most prevalent being the FM-2 which was built under license by General Motors between 1942 and 1945.

Restoration in process, 2006

The author toured the National Naval Aviation Museum in Pensacola, FL in 2002. There are a couple of Wildcats on display of the older F4F type. A tour guide explained that these aircraft were recovered from the bottom of Lake Michigan where student aviators had left them while learning to land on aircraft carrier decks (see page 61). The guide explained that there are approximately 311 Wildcats still on the bottom of Lake Michigan!

Out of the Hanger at last, 2008

In 2000, the author travel to Seattle for a VC-93 squadron reunion and to visit the Museum of Flight. It was a great pleasure to see one of the squadron aircraft again and reminisce about old times with squadron members. It was a particular pleasure to view the restoration process and talk with the museum's restoration staff. They were a patient audience while the author regaled them with tales of flying over Okinawa in 1945.

Restoration crew, 2000